The Weimar Republic

1919–1933

IN THE SAME SERIES

General Editors: Eric J. Evans and P. D. King

LANCASTER PAMPHLETS

The Weimar Republic
1919–1933

Ruth Henig

London and New York

First published 1998
by Routledge
11 New Fetter Lane, London EC4P 4EE
Simultaneously published in the USA and Canada
by Routledge
29 West 35th Street, New York, NY 10001

© 1998 Ruth Henig

Typeset in Bembo by Routledge
Printed and bound in Great Britain by Clays Ltd, St Ives plc

British Library Cataloguing in Publication Data
A catalogue record for this book is available from the British Library

Library of Congress Cataloging-in-Publication Data
Henig, Ruth B. (Ruth Beatrice)
The Weimar Republic, 1919–1933 / Ruth Henig.
(Lancaster pamphlets)
Includes bibliographical references.
1. Germany – Politics and government – 1918–1933. 2. Germany –
Economic policy – 1918–1933. 3. Germany – Social conditions – 1918
– 1933. 4. National socialism. 5. Germany – Historiography – History
– 20th century. I. Title. II. Series.
DD240.H42   1998
943.085–dc21   98–17122

ISBN 0–415–13284–3

Contents

Foreword

Lancaster Pamphlets offer concise and up-to-date accounts of major historical topics, primarily for the help of students preparing for Advanced Level examinations, though they should also be of value to those pursuing introductory courses in universities and other institutions of higher education. Without being all-embracing, their aims are to bring some of the central themes or problems confronting students and teachers into sharper focus than the textbook writer can hope to do; to provide the reader with some of the results of recent research which the textbook may not embody; and to stimulate thought about the whole interpreation of the topic under discussion.

Preface

Nearly fifty years after its unification in 1871, the German Empire was abruptly changed into a parliamentary republic. This major transformation came about as a direct result of German defeat in the First World War, a war which had serious economic and social consequences not just for Germany but for all of the European powers directly involved. Germany's first attempt at democracy therefore took place in extremely difficult circumstances, in a country which had experienced the impact of rapid modernisation and industrial expansion in the decades since 1870. Almost before it was proclaimed, the new republic found itself engulfed in revolution; within months it was saddled with a bitterly resented peace treaty.

Clearly the prospects for the establishment of a stable democratic regime in Germany after 1918 were not good. However, is it therefore valid to draw the conclusion that the Weimar Republic was 'doomed from the outset', its establishment 'a gamble which stood virtually no chance of success'? Or did the new democratic system gradually gain in strength and in support after a shaky start, only to be swept away in the economic hurricane unleashed by the Wall Street crash of 1929?

The debates about the prospects for survival of Weimar democracy are inevitably made much more contentious because of the Nazi regime which followed it. Given what we now know about the enormous crimes against humanity committed by the Third Reich, the question naturally arises as to whether Hitler's accession to power and the one-party rule which he established so rapidly could have been avoided. To what extent was the Weimar Republic deliberately and selfishly betrayed by influential interest groups seeking Hitler's support to preserve their own vested interests and influence? How valid is it to argue instead that Hitler was voted into power by a mass electorate ironically created by Weimar democracy but totally disillusioned by a decade of party bickering and political compromises, and radicalised by wage cuts and soaring unemployment?

This pamphlet will examine the establishment and operation of the Weimar Republic and consider both the long-term and short-term causes of its collapse. The first chapter will focus on the birth of the regime and the immediate problems it faced, and will examine the political structures which were established under the new democratic constitution. The early years of crisis, culminating in the invasion of the Ruhr and the spectacular collapse of the German currency, will be the focus of the second chapter, which will conclude with the Dawes settlement and the stabilisation of the regime. Chapter 3 will consider the extent to which the Weimar Republic established its authority between 1924 and 1929, and the nature and strength of the challenges which faced it by the late 1920s. Chapter 4 will then consider the impact of the great depression and the factors which contributed to the dramatic political rise of the Nazi Party, culminating in Hitler's appointment as Chancellor in January 1933.

Not surprisingly, there have been many vigorous debates amongst historians since the second world war about key episodes and issues which faced the new regime. Chapter 5 takes a brief look at some of the major areas of conflict and disagreement in an attempt to illuminate the variety of interpretations and of arguments which have been advanced in recent years. Inevitably there will be a range of different views about the main factors responsible for the failure of Germany's first experiment with democracy. The aim of this final chapter is to provide the basis for informed debate and discussion on Weimar Germany, to enable students to formulate their own judgements and historical interpretations.

My interest in Weimar Germany was first awakened as a child, when my father recounted to me his vivid impressions of the impact of the First World War in Upper Silesia, the shock of the collapse of the currency in 1923 and the growing tensions of the early 1930s. My mother was truly a Weimar baby, born in East Prussia in January 1920, and longing from an early age to savour the attractions of

Berlin rather than the quiet rural life of sleepy Hohenstein. This book is dedicated to my father, in fond memory of my mother, who died as it was being written.

Chronology

1918

9 November	Proclamation of the Republic
10 November	'Council of People's Representatives' formed by SPD and USPD representatives; pact agreed between Ebert and military leadership under Groener
11 November	Armistice signed
15 November	Agreement between heavy industry and trade unions to form a *Zentralarbeitsgemeinschaft*
16–20 November	Reich Congress of Councils meets in Berlin
29 December	USPD leaves Council of People's Representatives

1919

1 January	Founding congress of KPD
5–12 January	'Spartacus uprising'
19 January	Elections to National Assembly
11 February	Friedrich Ebert Reich President
13 February (–20 June)	Scheidemann (SPD) cabinet: Weimar Coalition (SPD, Centre, DDP)

21 June(–26 March 1920)	Bauer (SPD) cabinet: Weimar Coalition (SPD, Centre, DDP)
28 June	Versailles Peace Treaty signed
11 August	Weimar constitution signed

1920

13–17 March	Kapp putsch and general strike
March/April	Fighting between 'Red Ruhr Army' and Freikorps/Reichswehr
19 March	US Senate fails to ratify Versailles Treaty
27 March (–8 June)	Müller (SPD) cabinet I: Weimar Coalition (SPD, Centre, DDP)
6 June	Reichstag elections: Weimar Coalition defeated
25 June (–4 May 1921)	Fehrenbach (Centre) cabinet: Centre, DDP DVP
4–7 December	Left wing of USPD joins KPD

1921

20 March	Plebiscite in Upper Silesia
2 May	Fighting breaks out in Upper Silesia
5 May	London ultimatum on German reparations payments
10 May (–14 November 1922)	Wirth (Centre) cabinets I and II: SPD, Centre, DDP
26 August	Matthias Erzberger murdered

1922

16 April	Germany and Soviet Russia sign Rapallo Treaty during world economic conference at Genoa
24 June	Walther Rathenau murdered
18 July	Law for the Protection of the Republic
12 November (–12 August 1923)	Cuno (non-party) cabinet: Centre, DDP, DVP

1923

11 January	France occupies Ruhr
13 August (–23 November)	Stresemann (DVP) cabinet I: Great Coalition until 3 November (SPD, Centre, DDP, DVP); II: rump cabinet (Centre, DDP, DVP)
26 September	'Passive resistance' in Ruhr called off
22 October	Reichswehr units moved into Saxony; attempted Communist uprising in Hamburg
9 November	Abortive Hitler putsch in Munich
15 November	Rentenmark introduced to end inflation
30 November (–15 December 1924)	Marx (Centre) cabinets I and II (Stresemann remains Foreign Minister until 1929): Centre (BVP), DDP, DVP
30 November	Dawes Commission on reparations established

1924

9 April	Dawes Plan published
29 August	Dawes Plan legislation approved by Reichstag
7 December	Radical parties lose ground in second Reichstag elections of the year

1925

15 January (–12 May 1926)	Luther (non-party) cabinets I and II: *Bürgerblock* (Centre, BVP, DDP, DVP [DNVP])
27 February	NSDAP refounded
28 February	Death of Reich President Ebert
26 April	Hindenburg elected Reich President
14 July	Evacuation of Ruhr
5–16 October	Locarno conference

1926

12 May	Luther cabinet resigns over 'flag dispute'

16 May (–12 June 1928)	Marx (Centre) cabinets III (Centre, BVP, DDP, DVP) and IV (Centre, BVP, DVP, DNVP)
20 June	Referendum on expropriation of princely families
8 September	Germany becomes a member of League of Nations
8 October	General von Seeckt dismissed as chief of Army Command

1927

| 16 July | Labour Exchanges and Unemployment Insurance Law |

1928

20 May	Reichstag elections (gains by working–class parties, losses by conservatives and liberals)
28 June (–27 March 1930)	Müller (SPD) cabinet II: Great Coalition (SPD, Centre, BVP, DDP, DVP)
October	Ruhr iron and steel dispute: mass lock–out
20 October	Alfred Hugenberg becomes head of DNVP
8 December	Prelate Kaas becomes head of Centre Party

1929

7 June	Young Plan to bring about final settlement of reparations is drawn up
3 October	Death of Stresemann
24 October	'Black Thursday' on New York Stock Exchange; beginning of world economic crisis
22 December	Referendum to reject Young Plan fails

1930

12 March	Young Plan ratified by Reichstag
27 March	Müller cabinet resigns
30 March (–30 May 1932)	Brüning (Centre) cabinets I and II: presidential regime

30 June	Evacuation of Rhineland completed
16 July	Reichstag dissolved
14 September	Reichstag elections (gains by NSDAP)

1931

19 March	Plan for German–Austrian customs union announced
11 May	Austrian Kreditanstalt collapses
20 June	Hoover moratorium
13 July	Banking crisis in Germany

1932

2 February	Geneva disarmament conference opens
10 April	Hindenburg re-elected Reich President
13 April	SA and SS banned (until 16 June)
1 June (–17 November)	Papen cabinet: presidential regime
16 June–9 July	Lausanne conference: reparations ended
20 July	Prussian government deposed by Papen
31 July	Reichstag elections: NSDAP largest party
6 November	Reichstag elections: NSDAP loses ground for the first time
3 December (–28 January 1933)	Schleicher cabinet: presidential regime

1933

30 January (–30 April 1945)	Hitler cabinet

1

The birth of Weimar

A dynamic but deeply divided society

The unification of Germany ushered in a period of unprecedented economic and industrial expansion. On the eve of the First World War, the German Empire was Europe's most dynamic and rapidly growing industrial power. Coal production had increased since 1871 by 800 per cent, and the output of 277 million tons in 1914 almost rivalled the British volume of output, far eclipsing France's 40 million tons and Russia's 36 million. More electricity was generated than in Britain, Italy and France combined. In steel production, German furnaces turned out two-thirds of the European total, a greater output than the combined totals of Britain, France and Russia. German electrical and chemical industries led the world in their inventiveness and in the quality of their products.

Accompanying this massive economic growth was an equally impressive increase in population from 41 million in 1871 to almost 65 million in 1910, a rise of 50 per cent. By the eve of the First World War, around 60 per cent of this population lived in towns or cities as compared to just over one-third in 1871 and were seeking employment in industry and in handicrafts rather than in agriculture. By the end of the war, Germany's urban-based population was in percentage terms the second largest in the world, behind the United States of America. Such profound economic and population distribution changes could not fail to have the most far-reaching social, political and economic consequences.

The political facade of a united German Empire after 1871 concealed deep-seated regional divisions. The new constitution was based on a federation of twenty-five states, dominated by Prussia, which occupied three-fifths of the new territorial unit and contained three-fifths of its population. But smaller states clung tenaciously to their considerable financial and legal powers and to their distinctive local identities. Before 1914, there were no fewer than four German armies – those of Prussia, Bavaria, Württemberg and Saxony which were united only under the supreme command of the German Emperor. It was not until the First World War that one national army emerged, and only in the new constitution of 1919 that a single Reich army was firmly established under the supreme command of the President.

There were deep religious and ethnic divisions in the new empire. While the majority of the population embraced Protestantism, there were strong Catholic concentrations in the west and south of Germany, and from the outset the Catholic community operated politically through its own Catholic Centre Party. The Polish communities in the east and the Danish population in northern Germany also developed their own political and social organisations, and the French population of Alsace and Lorraine remained until 1918 totally unreconciled to rule from Berlin, a sentiment shared to a surprising degree by the indisputably German inhabitants of Bavaria and of Hanover.

Opposing political interest groups, shaped to a large extent by social and economic factors, also emerged strongly in the German Empire after 1870. The stronghold of conservative movements was to be found in the East Elbian provinces of Prussia, based on the large landed estates and their allied rural networks dominated by the old-established and well-connected *Junker* families. These powerful traditional agricultural elites were determined to maintain their dominant political position in the new Germany, but found themselves under increasing attack from more liberal forces representing the growing professional and commercial classes in the new empire. The pace of economic development which Germany experienced in the decades after 1870 greatly strengthened the liberal camp as against their conservative rivals, but it also introduced a dynamic new contender for political power, the Social Democratic Party representing the growing army of workers being recruited to workshops and to factories. As the population of Germany rocketed, the proportion of the German electorate voting for mainstream conservative and liberal parties declined from 60 per cent in the later 1880s to only 38 per cent in 1912. The Social Democratic Party, who gained a third of the votes cast in the 1912 election, had emerged as Germany's largest political party. In its commitment to sweeping, indeed revolutionary, economic and political change, it threatened the entire political and economic structure of Wilhelmine Germany, a structure the conservative elites were determined to retain intact.

Rapid social and economic change and modernisation compounded the growing political tensions. The agrarian sector increasingly lagged behind its dynamic industrial and commercial counterparts. As *Junker* estates struggled to meet the growing challenge of cheap food and grain imports, their political leaders became more determined than ever to uphold their political and social power, and to make no concessions to liberal or socialist forces. The growing middle class found itself torn in many different directions, some industrialists and professional groups wishing to make common cause with the agrarian social elites, some opting to continue to support the National Liberal Party or, on religious grounds, the Catholic Centre Party, and yet others wishing to move in a more progressive direction and offer some concessions to the working class. Political choice was to a considerable extent influenced by location – whether an individual lived in a large city, smaller community or in a rural area – and by occupation, whether in a dynamic, rapidly-growing sector of the economy or in a more traditional job. Yet by 1914 a substantial and growing proportion of the middle class felt itself to be increasingly on the defensive against hostile economic and social forces.

The huge growth in working-class power was perceived to be the greatest political and economic challenge facing the German Empire by the turn of the century, and many historians have cited it as one of the main spurs driving German leaders to contemplate involvement in war in 1914 in a desperate bid to uphold their supremacy. Yet the working class was itself divided by religion and by region, and the great mass of the rank and file was in fact more concerned to pursue immediate trade-union demands than to endorse revolutionary Marxist principles. Furthermore they were as susceptible to nationalist propaganda as were their social superiors and for the most part regarded themselves as German workers, or as natives of Bavaria or Schleswig, rather than as workers of the world.

3

Thus the regional, religious and social divides which had been such a pronounced feature of the German Empire in 1871 had by 1914 been overlaid by new economic and political divisions. On the eve of the First World War, Germany was a society in transition. Agriculture was giving way to industry, artisans' guilds to mass manufacture in factories, family businesses to commercial conglomerates and corporations. People were moving to towns and to cities, and in consequence their economic status was often at variance with their position in society, sometimes for the better, and sometimes not. Yet Germany remained in many ways a very traditional and hierarchical society, in which the occupational status of the head of the family defined and confirmed the position of all family members. As Thomas Childers has pointed out, 'family background in Germany was officially measured by father's occupation, not income. In a society where profession was listed in telephone directories along with family name, occupational status loomed very large indeed.'

Political and social change could not be kept at bay indefinitely. Sooner or later, working-class demands were bound to challenge the power of the predominantly landed ruling elites in Germany. At the same time, new economic elites were emerging, whose growing commercial wealth posed a different set of challenges to the agrarian elites. The failure to resolve these struggles for political and economic supremacy in the years before 1914 left a dangerous political legacy which had the potential to destabilise any subsequent regime. Furthermore, at the very time when a new political structure was urgently demanded, Germany faced defeat, and had experienced a lengthy and economically ruinous war, which left behind its own set of grave economic, political and social problems on top of the existing ones. It was not an auspicious start for the introduction of democracy.

The impact of the First World War

The German Chancellor, Bethmann-Hollweg, had worked hard in the weeks after the Sarajevo murders to persuade the German people that Germany had no choice but to fight a defensive war against the encircling Entente Powers, and particularly against reactionary, expansionist Russia.

The German population enthusiastically endorsed the government's decision to declare war, and on 4 August, 1914, the representatives of the workers sitting in the Reichstag under the banner of the SPD voted in favour of war credits.

This display of patriotism by the SPD Reichstag deputies had a number of fateful consequences. Committed Marxist members of the party were opposed from the outset to involvement in what they saw as a capitalist war against fellow workers in neighbouring countries. As the war dragged on, those who were ideologically opposed to it were able to gain considerable support for their views, and in 1917 they broke away from the main body of the SPD to form the Independent Social Democratic Party, or USPD. The divisions between the USPD and the SPD grew steadily wider as the war came to an end and added to the political and economic tensions which erupted across the country in the autumn of 1918.

At the beginning of the war, however, unity and patriotism characterised the mood of the country. The Kaiser was gratified that he saw only Germans, not parties; the socialists, whom he had dismissed as 'unpatriotic fellows' before the war, now appeared to be supporting it as enthusiastically as the rest of the population. This brief outburst of national solidarity and purpose remained strong in people's memories. Though it quickly gave way to stoic endurance and later to increasing social and economic unrest, the myth burned brightly of a *Volksgemeinschaft*, or people's community, bound together in pursuit of a clear set of national objectives. It was reinforced by the experience of soldiers in the trenches, drawn into close comradeship by the hardships and dangers they faced day after day. Throughout the 1920s, the image of a united German people selflessly pursuing a common destiny in war, on the battlefields and in the factories and workshops at home, was repeatedly contrasted with the allegedly shabby political compromises and self-seeking deals of Weimar politicians. It was a contrast that some extreme nationalists, and in particular the former First World War corporal, Adolf Hitler, exploited particularly effectively.

The scale and duration of the war quickly exceeded all expectations. The failure of the Schlieffen plan to defeat the French army within the first few weeks of combat led to stalemate on the western front, and to fighting on two widely separated battle fronts, in northern France and Belgium, and in Poland and western Russia. This was the military nightmare the German General Staff had sought so desperately to avoid. As the war dragged on, 13 million men in total were called up to serve in the German army, or nearly 20 per cent of Germany's 1914 population. Inevitably, there were large numbers of casualties, around 2 million killed and nearly 5 million wounded. Life in the trenches or on the eastern front took its toll; even those who escaped serious injury suffered gas attacks, or severe bouts of frostbite. By 1918, the great German army was beginning to experience significant problems of recruitment and morale. Hundreds of thousands of soldiers tried to buy their way out of combat, or to disappear from view while home on leave.

Throughout the 1920s, the new regime struggled to support the millions of men who could no longer work because of their war injuries, the 600,000 war widows and around 1.2 million children orphaned during the war. These people and their families believed passionately that the sacrifices made during the war should be acknowledged and to some degree recompensed. But in the economic climate of postwar Germany, this was asking for more than governments could afford without heavy tax increases. The economic consequence of the First World War was to impoverish Germany: in 1919, real national income was only two thirds of what it had been in 1913, and industrial production had shrunk to two-fifths.

To pay for the war, German leaders resorted to heavy borrowing in the confident expectation that victory would enable them to pass on their debts to their defeated enemies. The immediate effect was to trigger off massive inflation. In 1915, prices in Germany rose in one single year by more than they had over the previous forty-five years. By the end of 1918, the German mark had lost about three-quarters of its 1913 value. As price rises and in particular the costs of housing, fuel and food outstripped wage increases, unrest spread, particularly in the urban areas. By the end of the war, with real earnings having declined by between a quarter and a half in value, up to a third of the inhabitants of many major cities were surviving only by means of family support payments from the government, and the food shortages experienced particularly during the winter of 1917–18 drove millions to the edge of starvation.

But the misery was not seen to be equally shared. While millions suffered, a few were still able to afford ostentatiously luxurious holidays at fashionable spas or in elegant Baltic seaside resorts. It was said that 'everything is still available in any amounts at a high price'. By the end of the war, according to Kocka, the 'visible luxury of a few contrasted sharply with the increasing hardship of the masses'. There were other causes of social resentment. The importance of heavy industrial production to a successful war effort enabled union leaders to protect the wages and conditions of their members to a certain extent. Those on fixed incomes, however, who derived their living from rents, investment income or pensions saw an alarming erosion in their wealth by the end of the war.

The Russian revolutions of 1917 sent strong shock waves through the industrial centres of Germany. They fanned the flames of worker unrest and contributed to a total of over 550 strikes by the end of the year. In January 1918, more than a million workers were on strike across the country; the response of the military authorities who were now running the war was to redouble efforts to win an outright victory. To Colonel Bauer, one of Ludendorff's principal assistants, the choice was clear: victory would bring 'a long and secure peace, with firm, purposeful government at home'. A compromise or negotiated peace, on the other hand, would force Germany 'to drop militarily and politically out of the concert of great powers, decline into economic misery and drift towards a Bolshevik regime . . . '.

But with the United States now in the war, victory proved to be beyond Germany's capabilities. Instead of driving on to a glorious triumph, in the course of the summer of 1918 Germany's military leaders Hindenburg and Ludendorff found themselves facing a humiliating defeat. As Germany's allies Bulgaria and Austria–Hungary collapsed, her military options narrowed dramatically. She could fight on to the bitter end, risking invasion and significant territorial losses, or she could sue for the best peace terms available.

Faced with this stark choice, the German military commanders made two crucial decisions which had fateful consequences for their political successors. They decided that the most palatable peace settlement was likely to be gained from American President Woodrow Wilson's Fourteen Points speech of January 1918 which contained proposals which they had previously condemned as a front for 'imperialistic conquest in the guise of peace' and as serving the interests of 'Anglo–Saxon world hegemony'. And secondly they concluded that a civilian-based government would have more chance of securing a relatively lenient peace than a military one. Accordingly, the Reichstag leaders of those parties which had supported a peace resolution in July 1917 were suddenly transformed in late September 1918 from national traitors to responsible ministers, commanded by the desperate military authorities to take over the reins of government under the chancellorship of Prince Max of Baden and to sue for peace on the basis of Wilson's Fourteen Points.

Though the German army had been on the retreat since the late spring of 1918, it was still surviving in reasonable order, and had not yet been forced back into Germany. In handing over responsibility to the political parties at this crucial point in time, Ludendorff proved himself to be far more politically astute than the politicians. He adroitly shifted the blame for defeat onto their shoulders. As he explained to his military staff: 'I have advised His Majesty to bring those groups into the government whom we have in the main to thank for the fact that matters have reached this pass. . . . Let them now conclude the peace that has to be negotiated. Let them eat the broth they have prepared for us.' Thus the highest military authorities in Germany were already accusing the liberal, centre and left-wing party leaders of causing defeat by their demand for a negotiated peace in 1917 and by their refusal to give the army all-out support. It was not long before nationalist groups throughout Germany were elaborating on this 'stab in the back' administered by pacifists and socialists to the valiant army in the field, and asserting that defeat could have been averted, even victory secured, had it not been for the mood of defeatism and the sparks of revolution deliberately fanned by traitors at home.

The German revolution of 1918–19

The six months from October 1918 to March 1919 witnessed turbulent revolutionary activity across Germany, fierce struggles between socialists and nationalists and moves to establish a new constitutional state. This period is referred to as the 'German revolution', but in fact there were three different revolutionary processes in train, each with its own aims and agenda.

There were first of all those seeking far-reaching constitutional changes, initially seeking to reform the monarchy and make it more accountable to Parliament, but then, after the abdication of the Kaiser, in early November 1918, pressing for the setting up of a Constitutional Assembly to pave the way for a democratic republic. These were the aims of the Reichstag leaders entrusted with the task of negotiating a peace with President Wilson, broadly supported by the Catholic Centre, Progressive Liberal and Social Democratic parties.

However, the reluctance of the Kaiser to accept any changes, and an ill-judged attempt by the admiralty to order a last-ditch naval challenge by the High Seas Fleet to the British navy triggered off a second more radical revolutionary process. It seemed to the sailors at Kiel and to the war-weary workers and their families across the country that the authorities were intent on prolonging the war; as the peace negotiations dragged on, there was a mutiny at the big Kiel naval base, which led to the setting up of a sailors' council. Within days, in the first week of November, similar councils appeared at Wilhelmshaven, in Hamburg and Cologne. Soon workers' and soldiers' councils were to be found in towns and cities across Germany, demanding peace and assuming control of local food supplies and services. Some of these bodies were indeed very radical, and modelled themselves closely on the Russian soviets of 1917. Yet others came into being spontaneously in an effort to speed the end of the war and to defend the interests of the local community against unpopular measures ordered by government officials. How great the revolutionary threat of this council or *Räte* movement actually was is still hotly disputed by historians, but the suddenness with which it erupted, and the nation-wide scale and wide scope of its aims appeared very menacing to large sections of the population. Many nationalists, and even those pressing for constitutional reforms, were alarmed by what they perceived as 'Russian solutions' being put forward for German problems and consequently sought to challenge and to undermine the authority of the councils.

The third element of the revolutionary situation was provided by left-wing, avowedly Marxist, socialists who saw in the ending of the war their chance to overthrow the forces of capitalism and to establish a workers' state. They had already broken away from the majority SPD Party in 1917 because of their opposition to the war; now they seized the opportunity to drive forward the workers' revolution in the major cities and in the disaffected regions of Germany, either by harnessing the *Räte* movement to their cause or by directly organising massive strikes and demonstrations by workers. In Bavaria, on 7–8 November, Kurt Eisner and his followers, having seized control of the city of Munich, proclaimed a Bavarian Republic. In Berlin, Karl Liebknecht and Rosa Luxemburg worked to fan the flames of revolution and to gain the support of the disaffected masses for the proclamation of a Marxist state. Having established a left-wing splinter group, the Spartacus League, they were to rename themselves the German Communist Party in January 1919.

It is perhaps easiest to outline the course of the revolution in three distinct chronological phases. The first phase, from October to 11 November 1919, saw the outbreak of disturbances, as the new Chancellor, Max of Baden, opened negotiatiations with Woodrow Wilson for a peace settlement based on the Fourteen Points. When Wilson insisted on assurances that those who had been responsible for prosecuting the war would resign and negotiations would be conducted by new civilian leaders, Prince Max sought to persuade an extremely reluctant Kaiser to agree to far-reaching constitutional reforms, and, as mutinies and disorder spread, to abdicate. It was only on 9 November that the Kaiser finally agreed to leave Germany for what he regarded as a temporary flight to Holland – an exile which in fact lasted until his death in 1941.

The same day, Prince Max handed over his powers to the leader of the SPD Party, Frederick Ebert. An hour later, the SPD leadership proclaimed the establishment of a new democratic republic. But not far away, in the same city of Berlin, Karl Liebknecht was about to proclaim a new socialist republic and to appeal for support from the revolutionary masses. It was not possible for the SPD to exercise effective authority unless they had the backing of at least some of the independent socialists. Thus a Council of People's Commissars was formed, consisting of three SPD leaders and three from the USPD, in a conscious bid to outmanoeuvre the Berlin Revolutionary Shop Stewards who were working to bring about a revolutionary uprising in the capital city. For Ebert, the aim was clear: to stabilise the political situation sufficiently to enable elections to take place as soon as possible for a National Assembly. This body would then be entrusted with the task of drawing up a constitution for the new republic.

In this aim, Ebert had the full support of the government officials, local civil servants and industrialists who had witnessed the onset of revolution with growing horror. But more significantly, a telephone call from General Groener at military headquarters assured him of the full support of the army high command in order to facilitate the orderly retreat and smooth demobilisation of the German army. General Groener correctly surmised that Ebert was as anxious as the army authorities to defeat the Bolshevik challenge which threatened to spread revolution through the major urban centres of Germany, and that he needed at least some military assistance to restore order. The message of support from the army was swiftly followed by the announcement of peace. That same weekend, on Sunday 11 November, the Armistice was signed between German and allied representatives, and the First World War officially came to an end.

The second phase of the revolution spanned the period from the signing of the Armistice to the holding of elections for the National Assembly on 19 January 1919. It saw growing tensions between Ebert and the SPD on the one hand, and their USPD partners, who found themselves being continually pulled to the left by the revolutionary activities of the Marxist groups. While Ebert's concern was to ease the transition from war to peace for millions of returning soldiers and try to alleviate some of the economic hardship and food shortages facing large sections of the population, his Marxist rivals were planning street demonstrations and revolutionary uprisings. A demonstration of loyalty to Ebert in Berlin on 6 December was greeted by a counter demonstration organised by the Spartacus League, and in violent street clashes sixteen were killed and twelve seriously wounded. Far more serious clashes took place in January, as the Spartacists unleashed their revolutionary uprising in an attempt to overthrow the government. The uprising was crushed by the army, with the help of *Freikorps* troops, hastily recruited from volunteers organised by individual army commanders. With the situation contained, at least for the time being, *Freikorps* members took the opportunity, on 15 January, to murder both Liebknecht and Luxemburg. This outrage, more than any other event of the German revolution, ensured the implacable hostility of the Marxist left in Germany towards Ebert, the SPD and the new parliamentary republic. The events of January 1919 opened up divisions between the new German Communist Party and the SPD which could never thereafter be bridged. The USPD tried hard to manoeuvre between the two, but before long its members found themselves pulled either to the Communists or to the SPD.

Meanwhile, the soldiers' and workers' councils had held their first nation-wide congress in Berlin, from 16 to 21 December. While their social and economic demands were radical, they shared to a surprising extent Ebert's constitutional aims. Rather than opting to continue *de facto* government through their network of councils, they voted overwhelmingly to support elections to a National Assembly on 19 January. And Ebert's vision of a constitutional workers' republic had received a further boost in a series of far-reaching measures agreed between the leading trade unions and industrial leaders in November. The industrialists agreed that in future they would fully recognise the rights of trade unions to represent their workers, that they would accept legally binding wage agreements and a system of compulsory arbitration to regulate disputes, and that workers' councils should be introduced into all factories and workshops with more than fifty employees. Their most significant concession was to agree to the introduction of the eight-hour working day. The trade union leaders of the SPD thus secured most of the goals they had been pursuing for so long; they and their members were now more concerned to realise the gains they had achieved rather than to engage in further revolutionary activity.

The final phase of the revolution started with the elections to the National Assembly on 19 January and ran on until the spring. While workers' demonstrations and revolutionary disturbances continued, particularly in the Ruhr, in Bremen, Hamburg and Munich, they were more sporadic, and increasingly failed to mobilise mass support. Attention switched to the peace negotiations just getting under way in Paris, and to discussions about the new constitution. Above all, the outcome of the elections appeared to indicate widespread support for the political course which Ebert had followed thus far.

For the first time in German history, in the elections to the National Assembly in January 1919, women over 20 were able to vote alongside men for their chosen candidates, who were to be elected by a system of proportional representation. There was a turn-out of 83 per cent of those eligible to vote, despite appeals by the Communist Part to workers to boycott the elections. Ebert's SPD Party secured nearly 38 per cent of the vote, with a further 7½ per cent going to the USPD. With the Catholic Centre Party gaining the support of nearly 20 per cent of the electorate, and the German Democratic Party (the former Progressives) securing a further 18½ per cent, there was a resounding majority for the parties whose leaders had agreed to assume the reins of power the previous October. Nationalist and monarchist parties won less than 15 per cent of the votes cast.

The new Assembly delegates gathered in the picturesque southern German town of Weimar which had been home to Goethe, Schiller and Liszt. Berlin was considered too dangerous a venue, with revolutionary forces still strongly in evidence, though gradually declining in force. The Assembly opened on 9 February 1919, and two days later Ebert was elected by delegates as the first President of the new republic, gaining 277 votes out of a possible 379. A cabinet was formed, with ministers drawn from the Social Democrat, Catholic Centre and Democrat parties. A constitutional lawyer from the Democrat Party, the Jewish deputy Hugo Preuss, was entrusted with the task of drafting a constitution.

With the acceptance of the constitution by the National Assembly in July, by 262 votes to 75, the German revolution had effectively come to an end. Its constitutional aims had certainly been fully realised, but the more far-reaching social and economic goals of the council movement had not resulted in the wholesale removal of the existing economic or social structures. A Marxist revolution had been prevented, and many left-wing leaders had been murdered, including Kurt Eisner in Bavaria in February. Uprisings continued in militant industrial centres for several months, culminating in a serious disturbance in the Ruhr in 1920 and in communist-led revolts in Hamburg and in central Germany in 1921. But Germany did not succumb to the forces of communism, much to the disappointment of the Bolshevik regime in Russia. On the contrary, the forces of reaction and of strident nationalism made a swift recovery and emerged by 1920 as the most potent enemies of the new republic.

The Weimar constitution

The new constitution attempted a careful balance of political forces, and consisted of a number of compromises. Germany remained a federal, rather than a unitary state, but the existing powers of the individual states were reduced, particularly in the financial sphere. In future the government was to be allowed to levy direct taxes on income and capital, leaving the individual states only powers of indirect taxation. Though their financial independence was thus severely restricted, the states still retained the power to borrow freely, and the police, local government officials, teachers and judges remained under their regional authority.

The individual states were represented in an Upper Chamber or Reichsrat. Though they could in theory veto the legislation of the Lower Chamber or Reichstag, this veto could be overridden by a two-thirds vote of the Lower Chamber or by a national referendum. Thus individual states retained many of their powers after 1919, and Prussia in particular remained a strong and distinctive region in the new republic, but their collective influence was much diminished.

The new republic was to be a parliamentary democracy, with its ministers chosen from elected representatives to form a government based on party strength. All men and women over the age of 20 were eligible to vote, thus making Germany one of the first countries in Europe to allow votes for women. The country was divided into thirty-five huge electoral areas, and parties secured one representative for every 60,000 votes cast. The term of office was to be four years at most, and then another election had to be held. The army was to be placed under parliamentary control, as were all the great offices of state. The civil servants of the old regime were now to be answerable to new masters.

However, even parliamentary power had to be tempered. There was to be a President of the republic, elected for a seven-year term. The holder of the office was given wide-ranging powers to represent the new state, to conclude treaties and alliances, to exercise the right of supreme command over the country's armed forces and to dissolve the Reichstag. Under article 48 of the constitution, he could temporarily suspend constitutional guarantees and intervene if he deemed it necessary to restore public safety and order. Thus the President would check the Reichstag; the Reichstag would check the individual states, and parliamentary democracy would be safeguarded. Even the electorate was given the opportunity to initiate legislation: if one-tenth of the electorate pressed for a specific proposal to be submitted to the Reichstag, and it was rejected by deputies, it then had to be put to the electorate by means of a national referendum.

But the Weimar constitution was not simply concerned to build a viable political structure; it also sought to establish new social and economic rights. Every German had the right to work, and the new state would provide for those citizens not able to find a job. Every German had the right to a decent home. Workers could not be dismissed on grounds of sex, religion or political persuasion, and a National Factory Council was to oversee the network of agreements between unions and employers. The welfare of the population was placed at the top of the new political agenda.

The Weimar constitution was thus an ambitious and complex document. It sought to lay the basis for a modern parliamentary democracy, in which people would enjoy far-reaching political, social and economic rights. But it was introduced at the end of a long war, in the midst of a revolutionary crisis, in response to outside pressures and to the spectre of Bolshevism. As the revolutionary tide receded, dissatisfaction with the new political system was voiced more loudly. The flight of the Kaiser left a political vacuum which, try as he might, the new President, Ebert, could never hope to fill. As Mommsen has commented, 'the silent majority regarded democracy as an imported product implanted in Germany under allied pressure in 1919'. Wilhelmine state officials pledged their loyalty to the new state, but not to individual party governments. And the adoption by the new republic of the black, red and gold revolutionary flag of 1848 enraged nationalists, causing one *Freikorps* commander to denounce it as a 'Jewish rag'.

Not only did the Weimar Republic face an uphill battle in establishing its political legitimacy, but it also had to contend with the economic legacy of the war. There was no possibility of economic growth for many years to come. Instead, debts would have to be paid back and difficult economic choices would have to be faced. If the welfare provisions of the constitution were to be honoured, and poorer members of society were to gain a greater share of wealth, then this would have to be wrested from the richer classes in society, many of whom had already seen their income decline drastically during the war. Thus political antagonisms were certain to be reinforced by bitter economic and social conflicts over the division of a much smaller national cake. There could not have been a worse time for the inauguration of a new democratic republic.

2

The struggle for survival, 1919–23

The credibility of the new republic in the first six months of 1919 was crucially dependent on the nature of the peace settlement which its representatives were able to secure. Civilian leaders had been entrusted with the responsibility of conducting peace negotiations in the confident expectation that they would manage to secure from President Wilson and the allied leaders a more lenient settlement than the military authorities. As we have already seen, the German military high command calculated, correctly as it turned out, that if the politicians were unsuccessful the political odium of a harsh peace would fall on them and on the new republic rather than on the imperial regime and the army.

The chief German peace negotiator was its new Foreign Minister, Count Brockdorff-Rantzau, a former diplomat and member of the nobility of the Holstein region. He had won the confidence of liberal politicians in 1917 by supporting the quest for a compromise peace; however, he retained very traditional ideas about Germany's role in Europe and about what would constitute an honourable and there-fore acceptable peace for his country. To Brockdorff-Rantzau, and to other liberal members of Germany's aristocracy, Germany remained a great world power, without whose co-operation, particularly in the economic sphere, the United States and Britain would be unable to conclude a viable peace treaty. Furthermore, the menace of Bolshevism and the threat of its spread across Europe would surely make German co-operation even more indispensable to Wilson and to his fellow allies. In return for a 'just peace', based on the Fourteen Points and on some territorial losses, but with Germany continuing as a great European power and as a founder member of the new League of Nations, Germany would work with her former enemies to overthrow the Bolshevik regime and to reconstruct and rehabilitate Russia.

At the same time, the Wilsonian principles of national self-determination, which were fairly certain to result in the loss of Alsace-Lorraine and of the Polish provinces of western Prussia, could be invoked to justify to the allies the union of the German provinces of the former Austro-Hungarian Empire with the new republic.

As the peace negotiations between the allied and associated powers dragged on, and the German delegates were kept isolated and waiting impatiently in their quarters at Versailles, press reports could have left them in no doubt about the sort of peace which the allied electorates and their governments were demanding. After four years of fighting, which had resulted in extensive loss of life, destroyed large parts of northern France and Belgium and ravaged British mercantile tonnage on the high seas, the British, French and Italian prime ministers were in no position to contemplate a lenient peace. And even President Wilson, the most disinterested of the peace negotiators, firmly believed that Germany should have to pay the price for the Kaiser's irresponsibility in helping to bring about the war and for the manner in which the German military authorities had conducted it. There was thus a dangerous and unbridgeable gap between the peace terms which the Germans would find acceptable and the most lenient settlement which the allied and associated powers could contemplate. And even before the treaty was presented to the Germans, Brockdorff-Rantzau was threatening that if it did not amount to a 'just peace', then the Germans would throw in their lot with the Russians and work to overturn the whole European political and economic system.

The Versailles Treaty

It had originally been envisaged that once Germany's enemies had negotiated amongst themselves a preliminary peace settlement, the Germans would be admitted to the conference and invited to participate in a second stage. However, it proved so difficult for the allied and associated peacemakers to reach agreement that negotiations dragged on, until a complex series of interconnected compromises were eventually constructed. By the time the entire treaty had been put together, its authors were very afraid that any attempt to renegotiate individual articles, particularly in the presence of German delegates, would cause the whole settlement to unravel. Thus the German delegates were peremptorily summoned to the Hall of Mirrors in the palace of Versailles, where the coronation of the German Emperor had taken place so triumphantly in 1871. Here, on 7 May, they were handed a document consisting of 440 articles, and told that they had three weeks to consider it and to formulate any counter-proposals.

The German delegates, and the indignant German press, protested that they were being presented with a 'diktat', a very different situation from the one they had been promised. And on close inspection, the terms of the treaty were deemed to be so harsh that they generated bitter hostility and universal condemnation throughout Germany. The return of Alsace and Lorraine to France, and the cession of Eupen and Malmedy to Belgium were minor blows. More unpalatable were the placing of the coal-rich Saar province under the auspices of the League of Nations, and demilitarisation and occupation for fifteen years of the Rhineland, though at least the French government had not been successful in securing the river Rhine as the frontier between the two countries.

But it was over the territorial settlement in the east that most fury was aroused. A reconstituted Polish state came into being, which was to occupy a 'corridor' of land carved out of the German provinces of Posen and west Prussia. Henceforth, east Prussia was to be separated from the rest of Germany by this corridor, and the future destiny of the Prussian provinces of Allenstein and Marienwerder was to be decided after a plebiscite. The port of Danzig, a major Baltic commercial centre, was to be administered by the League of Nations, and in the south, Upper Silesia was also to be part of Poland.

To make matters worse, all Germany's prewar colonies were to be confiscated and administered by the League of Nations in the form of mandates. Germany's army was to be reduced to little more than the size of a police force, 100,000 men, to serve on a voluntary basis. Conscription was to be forbidden. The once-mighty prewar imperial navy was to be limited to six battleships, six light cruisers, twelve destroyers and twelve torpedo boats. Germany was not to be allowed to join the League of Nations for the time being, and she was to pay an unspecified, but substantial, reparations sum to the victors 'for causing all the loss and damage to which the Allied and Associated

Governments and their nationals have been subjected as a consequence of the war imposed upon them by the aggression of Germany and her allies'. Though the word 'guilt' was not mentioned, this clause 231 quickly became known in Germany as the 'war guilt clause', and was bitterly attacked as unjust and as 'a lie'. From left to right across the political spectrum, nearly all Germans were convinced that they had fought an honourable war of self-defence. They therefore saw clause 231 as a hypocritical attempt by the allies to seize the moral high ground while at the same time justifying the payment of punitive reparation sums. The German government was to make an interim payment to the allies and the USA of 20 billion gold marks by May 1921, by which time it was expected that a special reparations commission would have decided upon the final total of reparations to be paid. Employers and workers combined to denounce the allies' 'blank cheque' and the 'tribute payments of Versailles 'which would result in the future 'enslavement' of a generation of Germans.

German honour was further impugned by a clause demanding that the Germans hand over a number of 'war criminals' for trial by allied courts-martial. These included the former Kaiser, whose extradition from Holland was demanded so that he could be tried by an allied court 'for his acts in contravention of the laws and usages of war'. Though it was unlikely that the Dutch authorities would accede to this request, the proposal caused outrage to nationalists and monarchists in Germany, and even left-wing republicans were incensed.

In a debate in the National Assembly on 12 May, the SPD Prime Minister, Scheidemann, described the proposed treaty as unacceptable and declaimed dramatically, 'what hand must not wither which places these fetters on itself and on us?' He was supported in this intransigent stand by all parties except the Independent SPD spokesman who favoured accepting the terms since 'world revolution' was already on the march and would hopefully overturn the entire political order before too long. As German constitutional and economic experts produced a series of notes denouncing specific provisions, Brockdorff-Rantzau ensured that these were immediately made available to the press. His goal was to enlist the support of liberal and left-wing forces, particularly in the former enemy powers, against the harsh imperialist peace being imposed by the forces of capitalism. If the peace settlement could not be changed immediately, at least Germany could work to undermine and to revise it in the longer term.

The Germans were given three weeks to lodge their formal objections to the treaty. These were outlined at considerable length and submitted in great detail, but only resulted in two significant changes: the inhabitants of the Saar were to be able to vote on their future destiny after fifteen years of League administration, and there was to be a plebiscite to determine the territorial fate of Upper Silesia. The enraged Brockdorff-Rantzau and his entire peace delegation now threatened to refuse to sign the treaty. They were joined in this stance by the Prime Minister and by the Democrat drafter of the Weimar constitution, Preuss. President Ebert was also opposed to acceptance.

After heated debate, majorities in both the SPD and Catholic Centre parties voted to accept the terms, with the exception of the 'war guilt lie' and the 'extradition' clauses. Scheidemann immediately resigned, on 20 June, and Ebert needed a lot of persuasion to remain at his post. On 22 June, the National Assembly voted by 237 to 138 to accept the treaty apart from the two 'shameful paragraphs'. Many army commanders contemplated heroic resistance and 'death rather than slavery'. Soldiers threatened to mutiny if the treaty was signed unamended. Yet both the army and civilian leaders were well aware that failure to sign the treaty was likely to lead to renewed attack from the allies. The unity of the country and its very survival as a great power could be under threat.

Responsible army leaders like Groener, and a majority of SPD and Catholic Centre delegates were not prepared to run the risk. Instead, with heavy hearts, they sanctioned the signing of the treaty, while insisting that those who opposed this course of action made a public acknowledgement that they were acting from honourable and patriotic motives. It did not stop them from being the targets of abuse and of vitriolic attack for the next thirteen years. Already in 1919, the liberal theologian and sociologist Ernst Troelsch noted, 'the old legends about defeat due to Jews and SPD surface again. . . . Prof. X calls the peace a catastrophe which could only happen to a people whipped up by Jews and SPD . . . ' As if to underline the unpatriotic motives of those who were contemplating signing the treaty, the sailors on board the impounded German navy lying in Scapa Flow now scuttled the entire fleet rather than see it handed over to their hated enemies.

The Treaty of Versailles, including the reviled war-guilt clause and extradition clauses, were finally signed on 28 June 1919, by a new German Foreign Secretary from the SPD Party, Müller, and Transport

Minister Bell. Looked at dispassionately, it was nowhere near as puni-tive as the Treaty of Brest-Litovsk, imposed by the Germans on Russia in March 1918, or as the settlement the German High Command themselves contemplated imposing on the enemy. Germany was deprived of about 13½ per cent of her territory (including Alsace-Lorraine), about 13 per cent of her economic productivity and just over 10 per cent of her population. The most serious loss was 74 per cent of her iron ore, 41 per cent of her pig iron supplies and a quarter of her coal mines. Yet she remained a formidably strong economic power, despite the crippling costs of financing the war. Though she lost economically rich areas, she had no war-damaged provinces to repair. Her industrial and economic infrastructure, which had been modernised both during and since the war, remained intact.

The collapse of the Romanov and Habsburg Empires led to the fragmentation of eastern Europe, and to the emergence of small, weak successor states. Germany was no longer hemmed in from the east by Russia and by Austria–Hungary, and her strategic position in the heart of Europe was thus immensely strengthened. Furthermore, the war had weakened both France and Britain, and the real architect of victory, the United States of America, soon abandoned her role as the arbiter of Europe, repudiated the Treaty of Versailles, and retreated back to the New World. When reparations finally came to be fixed, in 1921, and Germany was deemed liable for payments of £6,000 million, this represented a significant, but not impossibly heavy, economic burden on the German economy. Furthermore, German denunciations of the treaty by this stage had born significant fruit. Many people in Britain and in the United States believed that Germany had been harshly treated, that the peace was 'thoroughly bad', and should be revised rather than enforced. The publication in December 1919 of John Maynard Keynes' *Economic Consequences of the Peace*, with its scathing denunciation of the economic clauses of the treaty as unjust and unworkable, had contributed to a significant change in attitude both in Britain and in the United States of America towards the settlement and towards their erstwhile enemy.

Within Germany, Keynes' attack on the settlement was seized upon eagerly as further evidence of the iniquity of the Treaty of Versailles, and as vindicating the German refusal to accept it as a 'just peace'. There was never any prospect of the peace settlement being assessed rationally or dispassionately, in terms of short-term losses and possible longer-term gains. Having to accept the reality of defeat, and

21

a treaty which both reinforced that reality and relegated Germany to the status of a second-class power was far too painful. Instead, in the new democratic political structure, parties vied with each other to attack the settlement, and to blame all Germany's political and economic problems on 'the shameful peace'. The Treaty of Versailles became 'the unifying bracket that clamped German politics together'. In such a climate of bitterness and despair, in which there was no shortage of mob orators vying with each other to heap odium on the peace terms, parties of the left and centre were bound to find themselves increasingly on the defensive against nationalists and supporters of the former regime.

It is difficult to conceive of any peace treaty acceptable to the allied powers and their electorates in 1919 which the Germans would not have found humiliating and unacceptable. The Treaty of Versailles provided ample ammunition for a series of sustained attacks by nationalists and militarists on the new republic, and was a significant factor in contributing to the recovery of right-wing political forces from the summer of 1919.

For the next four years, the republic was assaulted by nationalists on the right and by communists on the left. It managed to survive, but not to win the active support of the majority of the population.

The recovery of the right, 1919–21

Even before the signing of the Treaty of Versailles, a provisional new Reichswehr or German army of volunteers was being created, largely out of the more reliable of the Free Corps detachments which had sprung up throughout the country after January 1919. By June the government had at its disposal a well-equipped army of some 400,000, which was increasingly used to put down revolutionary insurrections in north and central Germany and in Bavaria. In addition to this, there remained several hundred thousand Free Corps volunteers, often students or demobilised soldiers, looking for action. They were involved in fighting in the Baltic region against Bolshevik forces, in Silesia against the Poles, and in street battles in Germany itself against Spartacists and communists. They were supported by a growing network of neighbourhood civilian militia organisations, student fraternities and patriotic clubs and societies, all of whom strongly denounced the peace treaty and vowed to defy its terms. As the government was forced to reduce the numbers of men under arms, to comply with the military clauses of the Treaty of Versailles, many veteran fighters took refuge on the estates of Pomeranian and east Prussian landowners, and were sheltered there with the connivance of the army authorities. Large local police forces were established, operating on quasi-military lines, highly equipped and drawing heavily on former soldiers.

As the government came under pressure to hand over stocks of weapons and ammunition to the Inter-Allied Control Commission supervising the disarmament provisions of the treaty, local army and police networks, supported by nationalist associations, tried to obstruct the process and took the lead in denouncing any hapless Germans who tried to co-operate with the allies.

The new government tried its best to discredit its intransigent military and nationalist opponents. The National Assembly had set up a commission of enquiry to investigate the causes of German defeat. The objective was to make it clear to the German population where the blame should lie for defeat in the war – on those who had authorised the major decisions of the former imperial regime. But by mid 1919, the army was recovering its strength and prestige. In December 1918, President Ebert had welcomed the defeated German troops back to Berlin as valiant soldiers who 'return unvanquished from the field of battle'.

When Field Marshall Hindenburg was called to give evidence to the commission of enquiry in November 1919 he drove through cheering crowds. Supporters had decorated the witness stand with a bouquet of flowers tied with a ribbon in the old imperial colours. Hindenburg refused to answer questions, and instead read a prepared statement, which concluded, 'Our repeated requests for strict discipline and strict laws were never met. Thus our operations were bound to fail and the collapse had to come. . . . An English general rightly said "The German army was stabbed in the back". The sound heart of the army is without blame. . . . Where the guilt lies is clearly proven. If further proof were necessary, it lies in the quoted remark of the English general and in the boundless astonishment of our enemies at their victory.' Hindenburg had in fact completely misquoted what Major-General Malcolm had actually said, but his words made wonderful copy for the press. He had effectively exploited the platform provided by the commission of enquiry to vindicate the achievements of the army, and, by implication, its leaders. The causes of Germany's failure to win the war clearly lay elsewhere.

The same message was conveyed by the National People's Party

leader, Helfferich, who, in a pamphlet, blamed 'all the misery and shame' suffered by Germany on the Catholic Centre leader, Erzberger. He had 'attacked German policy from the rear' with his sponsorship of the Reichstag peace resolution in July 1917, and 'thereby destroyed in the German people the belief in and therefore the will to victory'. His signature had sealed 'the miserable armistice' and during the peace negotiations he 'indicated to our enemies that he was willing to sign without conditions the treaty of shame and servitude'. Erzberger sued Helfferich for libel. During the course of the trial, all the accusations against Erzberger were fully aired and frequently repeated. Though most of them were found to be false, only a minor fine was imposed on Helfferich, and the court acknowledged his 'patriotic motives'. Erzberger was attacked by a student on his way to court and severely wounded; the student received a sentence of eighteen months' imprisonment for grievous bodily harm and was released before serving his full sentence. Once again, the bitter accusations of the nationalist right had more appeal to the German public than the sober denials of the centre and left.

Erzberger compounded his crimes in the eyes of his critics by carrying out a reform of the tax system in his capacity as finance minister. In an attempt to raise the income of the new republic, he introduced a progressive income tax with a top rate of 60 per cent. A corporation and capital gains tax, sales tax and various consumption taxes followed in due course. These taxes were bitterly attacked by property owners, industrialists and farmers on the grounds that they were delivering Germany's wealth into the grasping hands of her enemies via reparation payments. Any attempt to halt inflation and to restore Germany's finances was portrayed as unpatriotic.

A year later, while on a walking holiday in the Black Forest in August 1921, Erzberberger was murdered by two ex-army officers who were members of a clandestine nationalist organisation. They were helped to escape to Hungary via Munich, and remained there until 1933 when they returned to Germany. Only some of those implicated in the crime or facilitating the escape were brought to trial, and they were acquitted. It was observed that 'thousands celebrated openly, shamelessly'. Less than a year later, even more outrageously, the Foreign Minister, Rathenau, one of Germany's leading industrialists and a Jew, was assassinated by two young ex-officers from the same organisation, who subsequently committed suicide.

Though the Reichstag responded by passing a decree for the

protection of the republic, the problems it faced were very deep-seated. Important and influential sections of the population despised the new republic and all it stood for. Judges, army officers, aristocrats and professors took every opportunity to belittle its political leaders and their attempts to bring political and economic stability to Germany. And since many former officials, bureaucrats and army officers retained their positions under the new regime, they had ample opportunity to undermine it, while professing their loyalty to the German state.

Between 1918 and 1922, organisations on the right were responsible for 354 politically motivated murders. Only one of the perpetrators was punished, and then not with the death penalty. In the same period, the left mounted twenty-two assassination attempts. Seventeen of these were rigorously punished, ten with the death penalty. A study has shown that while the average sentence for left-wingers convicted of attempted murder was fifteen years, it was four months for those on the right. The latter were seen by the courts as motivated by patriotic sentiment and as a consequence entitled to a considerably reduced sentence. Another contrast in sentences tells the same story. A communist was sentenced to four weeks' imprisonment for denouncing Weimar as 'a robber's republic'. However, when a right-wing nationalist called it a 'Jew's republic', he was merely fined 70 marks. Such contrasts in what was and was not considered a serious attack on the regime clearly illustrate the enormous task facing liberal and democratic politicians in their attempts to win support for the republic from the electorate. They were hopelessly trapped between the militant socialist demands of the extreme left and the intransigent nationalism and conservatism of the right. It was relatively easy for industrial and commercial leaders, for army officers and farmers to attack ministers for being unpatriotic and for harbouring Marxist sympathies. Even if the charges were strenuously denied, opinions were swayed, emotions were aroused and the political climate inevitably became more nationalistic.

The Kapp putsch

In March 1920, attempts to disarm some of the Free Corps formations around Berlin, to comply with Treaty of Versailles military restrictions, helped to trigger off a military coup against the regime. It clearly had the support of large sections of the army, Prussian landowners, nationalist organisations and industrialists. Some sort of move against the government was being widely talked about, but the occupation of government buildings in Berlin by a mixture of regular and Free Corps units in fact happened very suddenly in the early hours of 13 March. Ominously, government ministers were told by military advisers that resistance on their part would be useless. A senior military commander, von Seekt, allegedly warned them that 'Reichswehr does not shoot on Reichswehr'.

The cabinet felt it had no choice but to flee ignominiously, first to Dresden and then to Stuttgart. But before leaving the capital, it called on Berlin workers to foil the attempted coup by means of a general strike. A proclamation was issued, exhorting that 'No factory must work while the military dictatorship of Ludendorff and Co. rules! Therefore down tools! Come out on strike! Deprive the military clique of oxygen! Fight with all means for the Republic!' While workers were being mobilised, civil servants and bosses adopted a position of studied neutrality, waiting to see how much support Kapp could muster.

In the event, the attempted coup collapsed ignominiously. Kapp and his fellow conspirators were unable to establish themselves as an effective government. Berlin slowly ground to a halt, as the general strike began to bite. Within a week, Kapp gave up and fled to Sweden. Those who had actively supported the putsch temporarily vanished from view. But the government had been severely shaken. The loyalty of the army had been tested and found to be severely wanting. Government officials had not acted disloyally, but neither had they shown much enthusiasm for the new republic. Its staunchest supporters had been revealed to be the workers of Berlin and of the other major German cities. Now they demanded their reward in the shape of stronger trade union powers, the socialisation of some industries, the organisation of worker militias, and dismissal of anti-republican officials and politically unreliable ministers.

Though the general strike was called off, workers in some industrial areas of Germany were impatient to continue their offensive and to turn it into an all-out class war. Red army units in the Ruhr led a workers' uprising of around 50,000 strong. Having overcome a right-wing coup, the government was now faced with a serious challenge from the left. It was suppressed, but only by employing the Free Corps forces which had been so deeply implicated in the Kapp putsch. The casualty rate was high – over a thousand workers were killed – and the bitter divisions between the militant left and the SPD Party were fatally reinforced. In many parts of Germany, self-defence groups had sprung up to counter the threat, alleged or real, from the left. But the real victim of all the political and social turmoil was the government itself. Support for the regime had been dangerously eroded, as the elections of June 1920 graphically demonstrated.

The 1920 elections and ensuing political instability

The first regular elections under the new Weimar constitution were scheduled to take place on 6 June 1920. As one observer commented, the results showed that the middle classes had moved to the right, while many workers had moved to the left. The three main political architects of the Weimar constitution all lost significant amounts of support. The middle-class Democrat Party lost 3.3 million of the 5.6 million votes gained the previous year. The Social Democrat vote slumped from 11.5 million to 6.1 million, though it still received the support of nearly 22 per cent of the electorate. And Catholic Centre support was nearly halved, plummeting from 6 million to 3.6 million votes, 13.6 per cent of the electorate. Looked at another way, the combined support for the three parties fell from 76.1 per cent of the vote in January 1919 to 43.6 per cent eighteen months later. They could no longer command a majority of the electorate.

Meanwhile, on the right the German People's Party increased its share of the vote from 4 per cent to nearly 14 per cent, and the Nationalists from 10 per cent to 15 per cent. And on the left, the Independent SPD vote shot up from 7.6 per cent to nearly 18 per cent. The results of the election were disastrous for the republic. Germany became, in the words of one wit, 'a Republic without republicans'. One could almost certainly paraphrase that it was also a democracy without a majority of committed democrats. Henceforth, Germany would be ruled by a series of weak coalition governments, destabilised by every crisis and unable to offer strong leadership. There were fourteen different governments from June 1920 to the end of 1932, and none of them ran their full four-year course.

It is easy to blame this situation on the Weimar constitution and in particular on the system of proportional representation that was adopted. In fact, though the voting system of the republic might have exacerbated political divisions, it did not cause them. The reality was that Germany in the 1920s was politically, socially and economically a very unstable and divided society, and this led political parties to appeal ever more intransigently to their own particular section of the electorate and to try to prevent supporters from being lost to other parties.

On the left, the Communist Party was at first no great threat to the SPD. However, in October 1920, most of the Independent SPD moved over to the KPD, making it a mass party for the first time. Henceforth, the KPD competed actively with the SPD for working-class votes. This meant that while SPD leaders in the Reichstag, who might hold ministerial posts in a coalition government, adopted moderate policies, the party rank and file endeavoured to emphasise its socialist credentials to maintain the support of blue-collar workers. Communists, meanwhile, drew attention to SPD 'hypocrisy' and compared the red-blooded communist commitment to workers' rights with the SPD's failure to secure greater benefits for the working man.

The party of middle-class intellectuals and liberals, the Democrat Party, saw its support drain away to the more right-wing German People's Party. The DVP proved to be far more successful than the DDP in attracting middle-class voters, in particular from the commercial and industrial sectors, but they in their turn found their position threatened by the more nationalist German Nationalist People's Party. This right-wing party, which drew on the support of landowners, farmers, leaders of heavy industry, traders and small family businesses, saw its support grow steadily during the 1920s, yet it too saw its voters wooed by special interest parties and by more extreme nationalist parties such as the NSDAP or Nazi Party.

The most broadly based party, which held nearly all coalition governments together, was the Catholic Centre Party. Its representa-tives sat in every government from 1919 to 1932, and drew support from great landowners and industrialists in Silesia and Westphalia, workers in the Ruhr and small peasant farmers of the Rhineland. Yet even this party had its rival vying for Catholic voters, the Bavarian People's Party, which broke away from the main party before the 1920 elections and attracted a fair proportion of former Catholic Centre voters in Bavaria.

With hindsight, historians have criticised the Weimar parties for failing to transform themselves into more broadly based coalitions with a wider social and political appeal. The reality was that in Germany, social divisions were very deep-seated, as were regional and religious affiliations. Parties found it difficult enough to adjust to a democratic political framework, after the highly autocratic rule of Wilhelmine Germany. To expect them to tailor their political programmes to appeal to a broad national constituency was to demand political skills of a very high order. It was much easier to maintain support by basing electoral appeals on established class interest, on religious affiliation and regional identity.

The more serious political problem was parties' reluctance to work together, for fear of alienating their grass-roots supporters. Leaders of the Social Democrat Party were reluctant to co-operate in government with their class enemies in the German People's Party, unless the Independent Socialists publicly supported them. When this support was not forthcoming, after the 1920 elections, the SPD went into opposition, to emphasise that they remained a socialist party dedicated to the economic and social advance of the working class. The pivot of the Weimar political system became the Catholic Centre Party, around which all coalition governments in the future had to be constructed. But their leaders also had to take great care: coalitions with the 'godless socialists' of the SPD were not popular with many of their voters. On the other hand, large numbers of Catholic voters supported progressive housing and welfare policies, and deplored the naked economic and social self-interest clearly visible in the political programmes espoused by the heavy industrialists and great landowners of the German National People's Party.

The Weimar political system was thus gravely handicapped from the outset by the range and depth of social and economic divisions which existed in Germany. The working-class vote was divided between the KPD, SPD and Catholic Centre parties. The middle-class progressives voted for the Democrat Party; the more conservative members and many commercial and business leaders for the Catholic Centre or German People's parties, and farmers, *Junker* landowners, wealthy industrialists and right-wing nationalists for the German National People's Party. In addition, on the right were a number of ultra-nationalist parties, some, like the NSDAP, combining a socialist economic programme with virulent nationalist and racist policies.

As unpopular political decisions had to be made, and the treaty terms carried out, the German electorate became disaffected with the main political parties and their leaders. Government posts were increasingly taken by non-party men who portrayed themselves as German nationalists untainted by political intrigue and compromise. For example, in 1922, a government of 'non-political experts' was formed under Dr Cuno, the managing director of the Hamburg–America shipping line. Though he had served as a member of the Reich Economic Council, he was not a deputy in the Reichstag. The message was clear: politicians, consumed by selfish ambition and party political concerns, could not be trusted to work together for the good of their country. With public confidence so lacking in the new democratic republic, the task of stabilising the economy and of carrying out the peace terms was an impossible one.

The struggle against Versailles

Between 1920 and 1923, politics in Germany was dominated by the ongoing battle between German representatives and the allies over the enforcement or evasion of the treaty terms. The major areas of contention were military restrictions, territorial losses, relations with Bolshevik Russia and, overshadowing all these, the payment of reparations.

The chaotic conditions in Germany over the winter of 1918–19, and the demobilisation of the army left hundreds of thousands of young men disorientated and thirsting for some sort of action. They found it fighting on the streets against political opponents, joining in nationalist fraternities or enlisting in irregular units which continued to fight after 1919 in the Baltic area and on the Polish borders. Successive governments faced great difficulties in trying to restrict Germany's military forces to 100,000, and in giving assurances to the allies that Germany was disarming to the limits stipulated by the Versailles Treaty. Large sections of the population resented the military restrictions and needed little encouragement to flout them. To begin with, open defiance was widespread. Then, as the allied Control Commission began more systematic surveillance of the size of Germany's army, the number of paramilitary organisations still in existence and the level of her armaments, the treaty terms were evaded by deception and by secret deals with the Soviet government. Large numbers of Free Corps units were absorbed into the military police, or were passed off as members of the Home Guards of the different German states. Meanwhile, the new German army, a small but select body of hand-picked recruits serving on a long-term basis under its commander, von Seekt, began a programme of intensive modernisation. Clandestine contacts established with the Red Army during the Russo-Polish war of 1919–20 enabled German units to try out weapons prohibited under the Versailles Treaty on Russian soil. Throughout the 1920s, the German military authorities continued to put the Bolshevik connection to good use, testing out aeroplanes, different types of poison gases and a range of armaments away from public gaze in Russia in return for providing military advice and training. Successive governments sought to assure the allies that Germany was complying with the military and naval peace terms. But in fact they were never fully adhered to or accepted. The German aim from 1919 onwards was to discredit the treaty and to bring about its revision, by whatever means. It was an endeavour shared by all parties, and covering all aspects of the settlement.

One comparatively straightforward way of weakening the treaty was by territorial revision, exploiting the various plebiscite provisions conceded by the allies. Between February and July 1920, plebiscites were held in Schleswig, in Eupen-Malmedy and in Marienwerder and Allenstein. While the inhabitants of the northern zone of Schleswig opted for incorporation in Denmark, and those in Eupen and Malmedy for union with Belgium, the southern part of Schleswig and the east Prussian provinces of Marienwerder and of Allenstein voted overwhelmingly to remain in Germany. But the vital contest was seen as being in the highly industrialised area of Upper Silesia. Both German and Polish volunteer units sought to influence the outcome by intimidating opponents. French troops, despatched to the area to keep the peace, openly sided with the Poles. As a result of all the disorder, the plebiscite was postponed until March 1921.

Of the votes cast, 60 per cent, 717,000, favoured incorporation into Germany. The remaining 40 per cent, 433,000, demanded inclusion into Poland. While German leaders claimed that, on the basis of such a majority, the whole of Upper Silesia should accordingly remain in Germany, the allies argued that they had a duty under the treaty to take into account economic and geographical factors as well as the local wishes of inhabitants in fixing the final frontier. Disorder flared up again, as volunteer Polish troops invaded the area. The British and French governments decided to hand over the task of dividing the region to the League of Nations, and an expert commission of four set to work over the summer. The final result, announced in October, was a bitter blow to the Germans. Though they received the largest share of the region in territorial terms, three-quarters of the rich industrial and mineral resources fell in the part of Upper Silesia assigned to Poland.

Anger over this decision, and continuing exclusion from the League of Nations increased the attraction of working with Soviet Russia to overturn the whole settlement. While some German leaders felt that they should seek to convince the allies, through a policy of attempted 'fulfilment', that Germany was economically too weak to carry out the treaty, others preferred a more defiant stand, working with Soviet Russia to frighten the allies into a wholesale revision of the treaty terms. The high point of this strategy was reached in April 1922, when Germany and Russia, both invited to attend an allied economic conference at Genoa, turned their backs on a general economic agreement and instead signed a treaty of friendship at nearby Rapallo. The scandalised allies suspected that the treaty contained secret military and economic clauses. This was not the case, but the prospect of continuing Soviet–German collaboration, in any form, was sufficiently frightening to strengthen the French resolve to enforce the treaty as strictly as possible, by military means if necessary.

French patience had already been severely taxed by the German response to reparation demands. While successive governments pleaded poverty and sought to postpone any definitive settlement, they did little to bring the German economy into better shape. After Erzberger's initial unpopular attempts to reform the tax system and to broaden its base, governments shied away from further economic reforms. An easier option was to continue with inflation, which assisted the government in bringing about a reasonably smooth transition from a war economy to a peace-time one. Though the mark was steadily depreciating in value from 1919 to 1923, the population at large was not aware of the real causes of the country's economic weakness and was encouraged to blame it on the allies and on their reparation demands.

In fact, governments were surviving by increasing the number of paper marks in circulation. At the beginning of 1920, the mark stood at one-tenth of its prewar value. By the summer of 1922 it had plummeted to one-hundredth. By the beginning of 1923, one old gold mark was equivalent in value to 2, 500 new paper ones. Debts of all sorts were being greatly reduced in value, but savings and fixed incomes were also shrinking rapidly in real terms. Somehow or other, the costs of the war had to be paid, but the German people were not made aware of how considerable they were, and by what means their governments were making ends meet without resorting to great increases in taxes.

Allied leaders suspected that their German counterparts were deliberately letting the mark fall in value so that any reparation payments would be made in devalued marks. There was some element of truth in this assessment. Any move by a German government to strengthen the currency would certainly invoke the charge that the German public was being deliberately impoverished in order to hand over tribute to the allies. Any move by a German leader to agree a reparations amount, however provisional, and to pay money to the allies on account immediately aroused a storm of protest. One newspaper was typical in proclaiming, 'we turn red with shame at the sight of a chancellor . . . boasting to the world how obediently he has done everything, how punctually he is paying . . . how conscientiously he is turning us into slaves . . . '.

The amount to be paid by Germany in reparations had not been specified in the Treaty of Versailles, largely because of allied disagreements over how much it would be possible to extract, and in what form. A German offer of 100,000 million gold marks to be paid in annual instalments over 50–60 years, free of interest, was rejected by the peace-makers. Their electorates were clamouring for far higher sums, though in Germany the offer was denounced by nationalists as 'insane'. The remitting of the issue to a Reparations Commission did not make an agreed solution any easier to reach. The one nation whose credit could have stimulated a European trade and industrial recovery, the United States of America, repudiated the peace settlement and took no further part in reparation negotiations. This left Britain, France, Belgium and Italy to haggle amongst themselves over the apportioning of potential German payments, and then to try to extract them.

The Reparations Commission had until 1 May 1921 to fix the total amount of reparations for which Germany should be liable. Earlier attempts to reach agreement with German representatives ended in bitter recriminations, and in allied threats to take sanctions if Germany did not agree to the proposals tabled. In the early part of 1921, three Rhineland ports, Düsseldorf, Duisburg and Rührort were actually occupied by allied troops. On 27 April, with the German representatives absent, the Reparations Commission finally declared Germany's reparations liability to be 132,000 million gold marks. A week later, the allies gave Germany six days to accept a schedule of reparations payments – 2,000 million marks annually plus 26 per cent of the value of her exports – or face an allied occupation of the Ruhr.

The refusal of the German People's Party to be associated with the humiliating acceptance of such terms led to a change of government. While their representatives left the cabinet, the Social Democrats returned, under the leadership of Joseph Wirth of the Catholic

Centre Party and Finance Minister Walter Rathenau of the Democrats. These two men took the view that they had no option but to carry through a policy of 'fulfilment', endeavouring to meet allied terms, while at the same time trying to persuade allied leaders of the impossibility of Germany, with her weak economy, being in a position to continue for very long with payments on such a scale.

For the next eighteen months, this strategy was pursued. It ran into fierce opposition from several quarters. Within Germany, nationalists objected hysterically to the payment of this 'slave tribute' to Germany's former enemies, and attributed all her economic ills, and her depreciating currency, to the continuing payment of reparations. Major industrialists, who benefited from the spiralling inflation, did all they could to obstruct reparations schedules, and at the same time, to avoid paying taxes. Meanwhile, outside Germany, the allies became increasingly alarmed at the plummeting value of the mark, and sought to bring pressure to bear on the German government to stabilise the currency. For their part, ministers insisted that stabilisation was possible only if it followed the postponement of reparation payments, in order to provide a breathing space for financial recovery.

As we have already seen, in June 1922, Rathenau was murdered by two right-wing extremists. He was the object of intense hatred both because he was a Jew and because of his willingness to face up to German liabilities under the peace treaty and to try within limits to meet them. His murder caused outrage across the political spectrum from the left to the moderate right, but it was only the most spectacular of a succession of assassination attempts – there had been an unsuccessful attempt on the life of the SPD leader Scheidemann only three weeks previously. In such a political climate, no government leaders felt able to acquiesce too openly in allied demands for currency stabilisation, reform of the financial system or for prompter payment of reparations.

In November 1922, Wirth resigned and was replaced by the non-party Cuno. He began to negotiate with the allies for a postponement of reparation payments for three or four years and for the raising of an international loan to enable currency stabilisation to be carried out. By this time, German finances were in a critical condition: the depreciation of the mark was rapidly spiralling out of control. Whereas in July 1922 an American dollar could be purchased for 439 marks, it required 7,589 by December. The index of German wholesale prices (1 in 1913) was 70.3 in June, but an alarming 1,475 by December. The French Prime Minister, Poincaré, believed that the

German printing of paper marks, which was fuelling this inflation, was a deliberate ploy designed to allow the Germans to make reparation payments in worthless marks. He declared that his objective was to force from the Germans 'productive pledges' instead of paper marks, if necessary by marching into Germany to seize the country's assets directly.

On 9 January 1923, the reparations commission declared that Germany had failed to deliver the required coal deliveries, in addition to earlier defaults on timber and telegraph poles. Though the British representative abstained, the finding was used to justify a military occupation of the Ruhr. In the course of the following week, French and Belgian troops marched over the border and into the industrial heartland of the Ruhr.

The occupation of the Ruhr, 1923–4

The aim of the occupation, as far as the French government was concerned, was to force Germany to acknowledge defeat and to carry out the peace terms, specifically the payment of reparations. Payment in kind, of coal, timber and the like, was to be seized at source. If the invasion triggered off an economic crisis or fanned the flames of separatism in the Rhineland or in Bavaria, so much the better. Anything that weakened Germany and thereby contributed to French security in the future was seen as a positive outcome. Though the British government did not actively support the military occupation, it took no steps to oppose it, watching from the sidelines as the French invasion triggered off a major crisis for the Weimar Republic.

The government's first response to the occupation was to declare a policy of 'passive resistance'. Industrialists and civil servants were ordered not to hand over coal stocks or to obey any French instructions. A general strike was declared in the Ruhr area, and was underwritten by the government, who continued to pay the wages and salaries of workers and of public employees by printing yet more money. Credit was extended to industrialists to keep their factories and mines solvent, as production ceased. But the loss of tax revenues and of export earnings added to the already enormous pressures on the government's finances. Within six months, the German currency had collapsed completely. In August, a dollar cost 4.6 million marks. Three months later, in the worst of the hyper-inflation, it cost an almost unimaginable 4,000 billion marks. The entire internal war debt of Germany, 154 billion marks, was now worth a mere 15.4 pfennigs!

To enable wages to continue to be paid, and commodities to be purchased, 133 printing offices and 1,783 machines were by this stage churning out paper notes for the Reichsbank. Over thirty paper factories were being employed to full capacity. Everyday food items, such as loaves of bread, joints of meat and vegetables were costing millions of marks, or enormous piles of paper notes. While people with mortgages, or with debts, or who had access to foreign currency benefited enormously from the crisis, for the great majority of the population it was a traumatic and deeply disturbing experience. One German summed up the summer of 1923 as 'madness, nightmare, desperation and chaos'. By the time passive resistance was called off in the autumn, public confidence in the republic and in its leaders was at rock bottom.

By this stage, the new German state was in considerable danger of falling apart. Extremist groups were not slow to exploit the crisis for their own advantage. On the left, communists in Saxony and in Thuringia were working to lay the basis for a more socialist government. There was a communist rising in Hamburg. On the great East Elbian estates, Free Corps volunteers waited expectantly for a call to arms against the French, or for action against the left. In Bavaria, a host of fringe nationalist groups, including Hitler's NSDAP, plotted to increase Bavarian autonomy and to strike against socialism and against any regional or national government which made concessions to the left. And in the Rhineland, the French authorities seemed to be making some headway in establishing a 'Rhenish Republic' and an 'Autonomous Palatinate'.

It has been argued that, in this desperate situation, three men saved the republic: the leader of the German People's Party, Stresemann, the commander of the Reichswehr, von Seekt, and a little later, the Commissioner for Currency (subsequently appointed as President of the Reichsbank) and architect of financial recovery, Schacht. In mid August, as a result of a vote of no confidence in Cuno's government tabled by the SPD, a new government was formed, including the SPD, Catholic Centre, Democrats and German People's Party, under Stresemann's leadership. A forceful politician, with impeccable nationalist credentials, Stresemann was seen as the 'strong leader' who was prepared to take the unpopular decisions which were necessary in order to rescue Germany from her parlous state.

Passive resistance was called off on 26 September. When this provoked frenzied opposition from right-wing forces outraged at such 'treachery', a state of national emergency was declared, and the country was placed under martial law. Von Seekt now faced the possibility of a military challenge from Bavaria, and elsewhere, and a march by extreme right-wing groups on Berlin to clean up the 'Marxist pig sty', suppressing communists in Saxony and Thuringia on the way. A melodramatic call to arms was indeed made by Hitler in early November, in a crowded beer hall in Munich. But by this stage, von Seekt had made it abundantly clear that the army would stand firm against any such challenges. Hitler was ignominiously arrested by local police the following morning. Order was duly restored in Bavaria and in the rest of Germany, following which von Seekt handed executive authority back to the elected government.

Meanwhile, steps had been taken to deal with the financial crisis, and to replace the now worthless currency. A new unit of currency, the Rentenmark, was introduced, at a rate of 4.20 to the dollar, and obtainable for just over 4 million paper marks. In a surprisingly short space of time, confidence was re-established, as an ingenious way was found to underwrite the new currency, by means of a mortgage on all German real estate which would take precedence over other charges. The credit for engineering this recovery was claimed by Schacht, a leading democrat, who, as President of the Reichsbank from December 1923, later replaced the temporary Rentenmark with a Reichsmark based on gold.

By the beginning of 1924, it was clear that French designs on German unity had been thwarted, and that the republic had survived. But the occupation, and the response of the German authorities and of the general public to it had damaging consequences. Confidence in the political and economic system of the country was seriously, possibly even fatally, undermined. Large sections of the German population had seen their savings and investments wiped out. Pensioners and poor families on welfare benefits had endured great hardship. Workers had seen the concessions of 1918, and in particular the prized eight-hour day, repudiated. Working hours had been unilaterally extended by employers without extra pay, work protection measures had been relaxed, and union membership had halved from over 8 million to 4 million.

The stabilisation of the currency was carried through at considerable economic cost. It turned Germany into a country of high prices and low wages. Unemployment shot up, and farmers also suffered as agricultural produce flooded onto the markets. Stabilisation was followed by revaluation of debts, which caused more anguish, bitter disputes and social conflict. Eventually, economic recovery did take place. Political and social tensions subsided, and life returned to some sort of normality.

After the turbulence of its early years, the Weimar Republic appeared to be settling down. Its internal enemies had been overcome. Its external enemies were conciliated. American bankers were willing to offer substantial foreign loans. But did the regime really gain in strength and in legitimacy between 1924 and 1928 or were appearances deceptive? An attempt will be made in the next chapter to assess to what extent confidence in the democratic republic was restored and increased, after the extraordinary upheavals of 1923.

3

Consolidation and confrontation

1924–8: the 'golden years'?

1924 is seen as the year in which stability finally returned to Germany, after the storms and stresses of the early 1920s. The Ruhr occupation was terminated, and a reparations and loans package was agreed, after the installation of new left-wing governments in Britain and France. But though this ushered in a period of political consolidation and of economic expansion, underlying tensions persisted. Advances in industry and in commerce alarmed small traders and artisans; the bright lights and *avant-garde* cultural attractions of Berlin incurred the hostility of traditional communities in rural areas; the expansion of welfare provisions alienated farmers who resented paying the necessary taxes. If we look in some detail at the political, economic and social developments of the years between 1924 and 1928, we can certainly observe substantial progress and significant modernisation. Accompanying this, however, were continuing resentments and a growing sense of alienation in many quarters. By 1928, well before the onset of the great depression, serious questions were already being raised about the continuation of democracy in Germany.

Political developments

Weimar Germany had six different cabinets between December 1923 and June 1928. Four of them were led by the Centre Party leader,

Marx, and two by a public servant of rather conservative leanings, Luther. In all of them, Stresemann held the position of Foreign Secretary, and was the dominant personality in the government. But these were by no means years of political consolidation. Instead, government policies, and, in particular, Stresemann's efforts to enhance Germany's international position, were bitterly attacked both from the left and, more significantly, from the nationalist right.

In May 1924, the German people went to the polls for the first time since 1920. The results clearly revealed their coolness towards the republic and towards policies of conciliation and international rehabilitation – around a third of votes were cast for parties which had declared their total opposition to such policies. The largest number of deputies in the Reichstag, 106, now belonged to the German National People's Party, DNVP, hostile and uncompromising critics of Stresemann's conciliatory policies. They secured just under 20 per cent of the vote, fractionally less than the SPD who secured 20.5 per cent of the vote and 100 seats. On the far right, a new party calling itself the National Socialist Freedom Movement gained 32 seats, 10 of which went to Hitler's Nazi supporters. Rather alarmingly, this total eclipsed the Democrat showing of only 28 seats. While the Catholic Centre held on to its support, securing 65 seats as against the 69 it had held previously, Stresemann saw his People's Party vote drop by a third, giving it only 44 seats as against a former total of 66. On the left, the Communists signalled their appearance as a serious political force with an impressive 62 deputies.

A weak minority government, resting only on the DVP, Democrats and Catholic Centre deputies, now took on the task of negotiating an international settlement of the Ruhr occupation and related reparations issues. Ministers knew that they could count on the support of the SPD, but they were equally certain to face virulent opposition from the right-wing parties. The DNVP or nationalists demanded that there be no second 'enslavement' after Versailles. Instead, the treaty should be repudiated, and Germany should join forces with Soviet Russia in a bid both to increase her great-power status and to overturn the whole European settlement. They despised Stresemann and campaigned ceaselessly for his resignation from the Foreign Office, and at the same time they refused to work at either regional or national level with the SPD. Even cruder and more relentless were the attacks on government policies from the racist right. Less frenetically, the deputies on the extreme left were content to bide their time and wait for the impending socialist revolution which they convinced themselves was coming closer with every political and economic crisis.

Looked at objectively, the Dawes settlement, as it came to be known after the American financier who chaired the initial financial commission of enquiry in early 1924, was beneficial to Germany. The willingness of the Americans to be involved in negotiations facilitated the conclusion of an agreement and enabled reparations liabilities in the future to be paid via an American Reparations Agent in Germany. No final overall liability was set for payments, but under a five-year plan, Germany was to start paying a billion marks a year, rising to 2.5 billion. At the same time a hefty international loan was put in place to help to boost the German economy and to enable it to meet payments. German state property, and in particular, the railways, were to serve as security for the loan.

While the Dawes plan put in place some external controls over the German economy, it also removed any future threat of invasion or sanctions if payments for any reason were not made. And it proved extremely beneficial in terms of attracting short-term capital to Germany. Under the Dawes plan about 16,000 million Reichsmarks flowed into Germany, largely from the United States of America. In the same period, of the mid to late 1920s, German governments paid out 7,000 million Reichsmarks in reparations. Such a favourable balance of credit enabled German industry both to recover its prewar levels of output and to undergo significant modernisation of its factories and manufacturing processes. But the Dawes package was not seen in such a positive light by the right-wing nationalists, who continued to attack Germany's 'enslavement' to the allies and the humiliating peace terms accepted by those dubbed as 'November criminals' by the extreme right. None the less, in late August 1924, its different elements went through the Reichstag, with moderate majorities of around eighty votes on most measures. The final settlement was signed in London on 30 August.

Despite this success, the political basis of the government continued to be very weak. Efforts to broaden its party composition in the autumn failed, and as a result the Reichstag was dissolved and new elections were called for December. A noticeable improvement in the economy lessened the appeal of the extremist parties: the communists held on to only 45 of their 62 seats, and the National Socialist Freedom Movement was left with 14 deputies, most of them Nazis. While the DNVP gained 7 seats, the SDP gained 31 and Stresemann's People's Party 7. However, the formation of a broad-

41

based government was as difficult as ever. Inclusion of the DNVP ruled out the participation of the SDP. For the next three and a half years, governments were based on a 'bourgois party bloc' which included the Democrats, Catholic Centre, Bavarian People's Party, DVP and sometimes the DNVP.

There is little evidence that the German public warmed to the republic or to its coalition governments during these years. On the contrary, there was a strongly expressed view that the necessary political compromises and party deals were sordid and a far cry from the patriotic and orderly government of Wilhelmine Germany. Many yearned for a system free from conflict and from sectional interest, and hankered after the elusive 'national community' which they remembered from the early months of the war.

A very clear indication of public attitudes came in 1925 with the need to elect a new President. Ebert's term of office was due to expire, and he had come under increasing attack, from the left for betraying the interests of workers to big business, and from the right for alleged treasonable activities in the strikes of January 1918 and shady financial dealings. In an effort to defend himself from the latter charge, Ebert delayed treatment for an inflamed appendix, and as a result he died at the end of February 1925. As Helmut Heiber has commented (in *The Weimar Republic*), he was 'hounded to death by his enemies' and 'despised as a renegade by many of his old friends'. The parties now cast around for a replacement, and seven candidates contested the first round of the presidential elections held in March. Since none of them was likely to win an outright majority, the second round would be the decisive stage of the contest.

At this point, the Catholic Centre Party, Democrats and SPD united to back the former Centre Party Chancellor, Marx. In an inspired move, the DNVP now put forward as a fitting candidate of the right the former Chief of the General Staff in the First World War, Paul Hindenburg. By this time, Hindenburg, who had taken no active part in the republic's affairs, was nearly 78. He was extremely reluctant to stand, and only agreed to do so after the lengthy and insistent entreaties of his friend the former admiral and architect of the Kaiser's navy, von Tirpitz. Thus the 'centre/left' candidate was now opposed by a legendary war hero. On the left, the Communists insisted on putting forward their own candidate, Thälmann. He polled just short of 2 million votes, enough to deprive Marx, on 13.75 million, of victory. Hindenburg, with over 14.5 million votes, emerged as the new President. As Stresemann remarked, the German people did not want a President in a top hat, but 'one in uniform and with strings of medals'.

It could be argued that Hindenburg's election helped to stabilise the republic. Many regarded him as a 'Kaiser-substitute' and felt that as President he would be able to protect the country against communist agitators, socialist rabble rousers and unscrupulous Jewish financiers. Thus sections of the population who had hitherto placed little confidence in Weimar governments saw Hindenburg as providing continuity in the face of a succession of weak governments and saw him as a man who could be relied upon to safeguard national interests. Looked at in a different light, however, Hindenburg's election could be seen as a serious defeat for the republic. He was used to a situation of military command but the checks and balances of a parliamentary democratic system were totally outside his experience. His friends and confidants were fellow *Junkers* from the great East Prussian estates, and army and navy officers. While he would no doubt stick firmly to the constitution, his presidential powers were considerable and could, in an emergency, be extremely far reaching. As E. J. Feuchtwanger has commented (in *From Weimar to Hitler*), 'One of the commanding heights of the republic was now in all but hostile hands.'

The most marked political trend of the mid 1920s was the decline of liberalism and what has been called 'the fragmentation of the centre'. This was clearly reflected in the Reichstag elections of 1928 when a quarter of the electorate supported parties which gained less than 5 per cent of the votes cast. Of the bourgeois parties, the DNVP lost nearly one-third of its seats, and the DVP, Democrats, Catholic Centre Party and Bavarian People's Party all declined in popularity. The beneficiaries were regional parties and special interest parties, such as the Economics Party of the German Middle Class, the Reich Party for People's Rights and Revaluation, the German Peasants' Party and the Christian National Peasants and Farmers' Party. Middle-class voters were clearly expressing their dissatisfaction with the policies and actions of the government parties. On the left, the SPD was rewarded for four years in opposition with an increase in the share of the vote from 20 per cent to nearly 30 per cent, and the Communists boosted their support from 9 per cent to 10.6 per cent.

The results of the 1928 elections did not bode well for the strengthening of German democracy. The effect of a decline in support, and the rise in the strength of the left-wing parties drove the moderate right parties and the DNVP further to the nationalist and racist right and made it more difficult for any of them to countenance a coalition with the SPD. Much of the electorate was disillusioned with the mainstream parties and was casting around for an appealing alternative. Though it was not obvious at this stage that the Nazis, with 12 seats, could command mass support, it was clear that a considerable minority of voters had not developed any strong attachment to the parties of the Weimar coalition governments. Nor were the parties themselves showing much success in becoming more broadly based, national coalitions in terms of class or religious affiliation. Thus as far as the political system is concerned, the evidence does not suggest that Weimar democracy was putting down strong roots. It was tolerated, for want of anything better, but it did not seem capable either of mobilising traditional loyalties or of attracting new ones, particularly from young, first-time voters, as we shall see. Its weakness remained that it was based on a series of political, economic and social compromises, and one by one these were all in the process of breaking down by 1928.

Stresemann's foreign policy

The position of the Weimar Republic in the mid 1920s was undoubtedly strengthened by the foreign policy achievements of Gustav Stresemann. This 'realistic nationalist', as he has been described, pursued a skilful course which entailed accepting some elements of the Treaty of Versailles whilst seeking support for wholesale territorial revision, mainly in eastern Europe. Yet despite his considerable diplomatic success, his policies came under increasingly bitter attack from political opponents in the DNVP and on the extreme right. Indeed, the more concessions he won from the allies the greater were the expectations he aroused within Germany concerning what could be achieved and the greater were the dissatisfactions with what were portrayed as the limited nature of his gains.

The difficult position Stresemann found himself in was symptomatic of the problems which faced the Weimar Republic. Unlike his critics, he was realistic about Germany's diplomatic situation in Europe and about the need to win the trust and support of her former enemies before any treaty revision could be secured. At the same time, he was as much of a German nationalist as his right-wing opponents, and shared many of the same aspirations, though he was more conscious than they were of the difficulties in the way of their realisation. As the leader of a major political party, the DVP, he had to present his policies to the German electorate with a clear emphasis on their nationalist appeal. Outside Germany, however, he had to appear as the apostle of German moderation. It is a mark of his political skill that he was able to achieve so much in a relatively short period of time, yet even he was ultimately driven to his death in 1929 by the unremitting hostility and personal attacks of his nationalist opponents.

All political parties in the 1920s were united in their wish for Germany to recover her status as a great power as speedily as possible. This meant in the first instance negotiating an early end to the allied occupation of the Rhineland, which was scheduled under the Treaty of Versailles to last for fifteen years, and also dismantling the controls which the allies had put in place to supervise German finances and disarmament. Once these immediate goals had been achieved, more ambitious objectives took centre stage, focusing on territorial revision and the recovery of former German land, particularly in Poland. After this, divisions opened up between those who wanted to press for closer links with the 10–12 million Germans living in Alsace, in the South Tyrol and in eastern and central Europe and for a speedy *Anschluss* with Austria, and those who felt that such aims were not realistic since they were certain to involve Germany in serious complications by incurring the hostility and opposition of other European powers.

In a bid to secure an early end to the Rhineland occupation and the withdrawal of the allied military control commission, Stresemann proposed to the French and British governments in early 1925 the conclusion of a Rhineland pact. After intensive diplomatic and political exchanges, a major international conference was held in Locarno, Switzerland in October 1925, and the Locarno pacts were concluded. These covered both the western and eastern frontiers of Germany. In western Europe, Stresemann accepted the frontiers as established under the Treaty of Versailles, and the continuing demilitarisation of the Rhineland. In return, the first phase of the allied occupation of the Rhineland would be terminated, and the allied control commission would be wound up once Germany had applied to, and been accepted as a member of, the League of Nations. She accordingly joined the League in autumn 1926, and the control commission left Germany in 1927.

As regards eastern Europe, the Locarno treaties were of a rather different kind. Germany agreed to sign arbitration treaties with her eastern neighbours Poland and Czechoslovakia to solve frontier disputes by peaceful means, but conspicuously she did not accept the finality of the frontiers in the same terms as in the west. Indeed, there is general agreement amongst historians that the Locarno settlement gave Germany 'a green light' for future expansion into eastern Europe and that, by agreeing to it, Britain, France and Italy were tacitly acquiescing in this possibility. Not surprisingly, the Soviet government, Germany's erstwhile accomplice at Rapallo, was alarmed by the Locarno treaties and especially by the German entry into the 'capitalist conspiracy' as they viewed the League of Nations. The German Foreign Office felt it necessary to reassure both the Soviet government and critics at home by the conclusion of the Berlin Treaty with Russia in 1926, and by qualifying the obligations Germany would accept under article 16 of the League Covenant.

The conclusion of the Locarno treaties, and the close personal relations which Stresemann established with his British and French counterparts, Briand and Chamberlain, were a considerable achievement for the German Foreign Secretary, and brought Germany back to the centre of the European diplomatic fold. All three statesmen were jointly awarded the Nobel Peace Prize in 1926. Within Germany, however, the Locarno treaties were attacked by nationalists for reaffirming the hated Versailles settlement, and for driving a wedge between the two great east European revisionist powers Germany and Soviet Russia. The Locarno treaties only scraped through the Reichstag by a narrow majority. None the less, they were followed in 1928 by German adherence to the Kellogg–Briand pact, whose signatories agreed not to go to war in pursuit of their national objectives. And a year later, the allies agreed to the total evacuation of their troops from the Rhineland, six years ahead of schedule.

However, little tangible progress was made in eastern Europe. Stresemann had stressed his nationalist credentials when he confirmed in a letter to the Crown Prince in 1925 that his objectives were to recover Danzig and the Polish corridor and to correct the frontier of Upper Silesia. (He was less enthusiastic about a union with Austria which, he felt, would bring complications to Germany rather than advantages.) However, it was not clear by what means such a programme was to be achieved. Large numbers of Germans shared von Seekt's view that Poland's existence was 'unbearable . . . it must disappear . . . ', but not all would necessarily back the fanatical nationalists who were prepared to advocate war, if necessary, to end Poland's existence as an independent state.

Stresemann's approach was to combine diplomacy with firm intent, to work within the framework of the League of Nations but to use Germany's growing economic strength to back up her demands. As he confided to the Crown Prince, 'All the questions that lie so close to German hearts, as, for instance, war guilt, general disarmament, Danzig, the Saar, etc., are matters for the League of Nations, and a skilful speaker at a plenary session of the League may make them very disagreeable for the Entente.' However, he had little to show for such tactics by the end of 1928, and German nationalists were expressing their impatience in increasingly bellicose terms. The improvement he had secured in Germany's position had the unfortunate effect of turning him into a prisoner of the right, and of exposing him to cruel taunts about his lack of progress with treaty revision. At the same time, crude nationalist clamour in the Reichstag and on public platforms throughout Germany increased the reluctance of Germany's new allies to agree to further concessions.

Economic recovery

Nationalist demands for more sweeping revision of the Treaty of Versailles were increasingly fuelled by Germany's recovery as a great industrial power. By 1925, Germany's industrial production had reached 95 per cent of its 1913 level, as opposed to Britain's 86 per cent. With the help of foreign loans, which flowed freely into Germany as a result of the Dawes settlement, Germany's productive capacity soared, as her factories and workshops underwent far-reaching modernisation. Between 1924 and 1929, German industry was rationalised on American lines. Industrial managers reorganised and modernised the means of production in their factories in a bid to increase the productivity of workers. Mass production was facilitated by a more organised division of labour. The result was a great expansion of output per worker. Miners doubled their output of coal, and the output of those employed in blast furnaces trebled. The American reparations agent operating in Germany under the Dawes settlement, Parker Gilbert, estimated in 1930 that the increase in Germany's productive means in the period since 1924 exceeded several times over the amount of foreign debt incurred in the same period.

Not all sectors of industry were able to take advantage of such growth in productivity. Heavy industry found considerable difficulty in increasing its markets. Steel mills in particular were only operating at 77 per cent of their capacity in 1927, as against 89 per cent in the mining and manufacturing sectors. But machine tool and electro-technical businesses, textiles and chemicals boomed and performed strongly in export markets. By 1927, Germany had regained her prewar volume of industrial production, and in 1928 figures showed her industrial output to be second in volume only to the United States.

Workers as well as industrialists clearly benefited from this economic boom. Historians have differed in their assessments of the extent to which their real wages and living standards increased in the mid 1920s, but there is no doubt that industrial workers saw their earnings increase substantially. Labour's share of the national income was 10 per cent higher in the mid 1920s than it had been before 1914. It is estimated that workers' real wages increased by 9 per cent in 1927 and by a further 12 per cent in 1928, making the German labour force the highest paid industrial work force in Europe. However, it should be emphasised that the principal gainers were mainly men, skilled and unskilled, working in large industrial complexes. Though 36 per cent of women were recorded as working in the 1920s, most of them earned low wages as temporary, manual workers, as domestic servants or in family businesses and farms. Furthermore, male unskilled workers earned more than skilled female ones. The one promising area for educated and unmarried women was white-collar work – more women than men took up the new opportunities offered by Germany's expanding industrial sector and welfare services – as secretaries, telephonists, salesgirls, nurses and teachers.

Workers benefited not just from an increase in earnings and a greater range of opportunities, but also from the state-backed wage arbitration agreements of 1918–19 which increasingly favoured the claims of workers as against employers. At the same time, their living standards were raised by a steady expansion in municipal house-building programmes, improvements in health care and a steady growth in welfare provision. Between 1924 and 1931, just over 2 million new homes were built, and a further 195,000 modernised. Germany still had a chronic housing shortage, but local councils had taken out loans to finance a range of new schemes, including the building of blocks of residences, and medical facilities. There were more doctors in Germany in the 1920s than before 1914, and the numbers of hospital beds also increased.

The government took the lead in increasing expenditure on social services from 37 per cent of total government spending in 1913 to

57 per cent in 1925 and to 68 per cent by 1932. Much of this spending went on housing and education, but increasing amounts were accounted for by social and unemployment assistance and by government contributions to pension and sickness insurance schemes. At local level, municipal and regional councils took out loans to finance an expansion in local facilities. Parks, stadia, concert halls, opera houses, gas and electricity schemes, road networks and sometimes even local aerodromes were established or expanded. Germany's cities vied with each other to become cultural centres, and to provide new attractions such as the cinema and the dance hall. Modern leisure facilities became established in this period, as cycling, hiking, sports clubs, public libraries and adult education networks attracted increasing numbers of participants.

The most modern and dynamic city of them all was Berlin, the world's third biggest city in the 1920s after London and New York. It boasted 120 newspapers and 40 theatres, and it offered its residents not just the latest flowering of Weimar culture in drama, music and opera but up-to-the minute American entertainment. While young people, the young-at-heart and progressives from all over Germany flocked to Berlin to be enthralled by its captivating movement and modernity, exaggerated tales of depravity and of corruption disgusted conservative-minded communities in more sedate rural areas. One Protestant cleric forecast gloomily in 1929, 'it is not socialism but Americanism that will be the end of everything as we have known it'. To some, and particularly to the young, America meant progress, excitement, and freedom from convention. To others it meant decadence and the undermining of traditional morality and values.

Thus by the later 1920s, the contrasting faces of Weimar Germany were very evident: expanding and lively cities surrounded by stagnating rural areas, and growing prosperity and rising living standards for unskilled workers and their families as against falling profits for farmers and small family businesses. While the economy of the Weimar Republic was undoubtedly growing in the mid 1920s, thanks largely to foreign capital, many sections of the German population felt strongly that they were not receiving their fair share of rewards. Indeed, considerable numbers of small businessmen and farmers believed that it was their increasing taxes and contributions to welfare schemes which were helping to increase the wages and living standards of workers in the cities while they were sliding further into poverty and facing rising debts.

The agricultural sector of the German economy continued its

49

decline in the 1920s as against other, more dynamic elements, and was Germany's major low-productivity occupation. Together with fishing and forestry, agriculture employed over 30 per cent of the population in 1925, but contributed only around 16 per cent of Germany's income. Though there were some very large landed estates in east Prussia, the great majority of Germany's farms were either small units of up to five hectares (51 per cent) or slightly larger ones of between five and twenty hectares (nearly 40 per cent). In the Schleswig-Holstein area, there was a considerable amount of dairy farming and intensive animal husbandry; in the south, sugar beet and other root crops were grown; the east produced grain, potatoes, rye, oats and wheat. But everywhere the fear was the same, that cheap imports would undercut more expensive German products and the cry was for protective tariffs.

The inflation of the early 1920s had to a certain extent benefited German agriculture by reducing debts, but stabilisation after 1924 hit German farmers hard. Overall in Germany, the tax burden, as a percentage of the national income, rose from 9 per cent in 1913 to 17 per cent in 1925. Between 1924 and 1930, taxes on agriculture were established at 3.7 times the prewar level. Farmers often found themselves borrowing money to pay taxes and to buy seeds, fertiliser and new machinery, hoping that renewed inflation would take care of their debts. Unfortunately, they were faced instead by revaluation, by continuing low prices of agricultural output on world markets and by increased foreign competition. Interest rates were high after 1924, and banks proved to be unsympathetic to their plight. Per head, the incomes of small farmers were 44 per cent less than the national average in the mid 1920s whereas before 1914 they had been only 20 per cent less. Put another way, between 1913 and 1928 farmers' real incomes rose by only 4.5 per cent as against a national average for all workers of 45 per cent. No wonder farmers felt that they were paying a high price for Weimar governments and getting few benefits in return!

By 1929, few farms were profitable, and high interest rates on their debts were a major cause of farmers' grievances. Over the winter of 1927–8, an agrarian crisis developed as wheat prices fell. As rural distress spread, peasants and small farmers switched their political allegiance from traditional nationalist, monarchist conservative parties to new, radical peasant movements. The agricultural crisis offered unexpected opportunities to radical right-wing parties, and the Nazi Party was not slow to exploit them. One of its Bavarian members,

Julius Streicher, claimed in October 1927 that 'the peasantry is without a fatherland, German land is sold and mortgaged to the international Jewish controlling power; today the peasant no longer possesses his own corn for he must pay four-fifths of his income in taxes, and woe betide him who does not pay, for then the bailiff comes'. A police report from north-west Germany noted, in January 1928, that 'in meetings of the rural population which were held in many places in the state of Oldenburg during the past weeks, the majority of those participating demanded again and again that an open-air protest meeting should be held . . . in order to give weight to the demands of the rural population . . . [and] . . . open the eyes of the state government to the masses of discontented who stand behind these demands'. The police listed the Rural League, the Farmers' Association, League of Smallholdings, Artisans' League, Settlers' Association and the Shopkeepers' Guild as amongst the organisations summoning their members to a mass demonstration which resulted in an outdoor meeting of some 20,000 disgruntled country people on 26 January.

What was extremely significant about the resolutions passed by this meeting, and no doubt by many similar protest rallies in other rural parts of Germany, was the identification of economic grievances with the political system of the Weimar Republic. With prompting from some Nazi speakers present, the meeting declared that 'the distress of agriculture is inseparably bound up with the *political misery* of the whole German people . . . parliamentarism which is corrupt through and through and a weak government are unable to over-come the German political and economic emergency. Let us do away with this Marxist-capitalist extortion system that has made Germany, our homeland, powerless, without honour, defenceless, and that has turned us free German farmers and middle-class people into poor, misused slaves of the world stock exchange.' And defiantly, and ominously, those present asserted that 'only when Germany is reborn in power, freedom and honour, led by unselfish German men who are not burdened by the contemptible policy of the last few years, only then will the German farmer stand as a free man on free soil serving the great German community as the backbone of our people'.

The German *Mittelstand*, that section of society comprising arti-sans, craftsmen, small shopkeepers and public servants was, by 1928, increasingly associating itself with the grievances of peasants and farmers. In smaller communities, the economic difficulties experienced by farmers quickly affected other tradespeople. The levels of taxation, markedly above prewar levels, the contributions to welfare services and increased bureaucracy infuriated small traders and business men. Furthermore, they found their prices and services being undercut by bigger urban enterprises, and their livelihoods challenged by a growing number of large, modern department stores in major cities and rural centres.

Thus a growing section of the German population joined with farmers and agricultural interest groups in the course of 1928 to lobby for more tariff protection, tax relief, cheap credit, a cut-back in state functions and expenses, sharp reductions in state welfare measures, an end to the eight-hour day, the protection of small craftsmen, an end to the 'pampering of big cities' and the payment of reparations, and 'a strong government led by a strong man'. Above all they demanded a return from 'the Welfare State' back to the 'Work State'. Their grievances were also increasingly shared by businessmen and major industrial leaders, who felt that their levels of profitability were being sharply reduced by workers' high wages and generous welfare benefits. Even after the depression had struck in 1929, business leaders were blaming the economic crisis not on international factors, but on clearly defined domestic ones: 'We have not only lost a war, but we have had a fundamentally new government, which has been concerned for 10 or 12 years to distribute charity to all sides, and that with a generosity which could not have been greater if the war had been won.'

It was sentiments such as these which led to the great Ruhr lockout of November 1928, when employers in the iron and steel industries refused to accept a binding arbitration award. Angered that wage demands were outstripping productivity, they locked a quarter of a million workers out of their factories to try to brow-beat them into accepting lower wages. The unilateral action of the industrialists not only angered the government but alientated the general public, whose sympathies swung to the side of the workers. Though the latter were unable to claim unemployment benefits, a majority of deputies in the Reichstag voted to provide funds to local authorities to enable them to support the workers and their families. The crisis was resolved when the government appointed a special arbitrator who produced a compromise solution which combined lower wage increases than the original award but with reduced hours. None the less, the magnitude of the crisis demonstrated the strength of feeling after 1928 against the Weimar Republic and its alleged 'partiality' to workers amongst industrialists, particularly in the heavy industry sector. Because labour costs were such a large part of their overheads, factory bosses argued that high wages and welfare taxes were driving them into unprofitability. As Dick Geary has pointed out, the purpose of the Ruhr lock-out was 'not simply to win a particular battle over wages but to challenge the whole Weimar system of state arbitration and collective wage agreements'. Though victory was not won immediately, the nature of the challenge was a fundamental one, which, once the depression had struck, was to gain widespread support.

Opposition to the Weimar system of government by 1928

In addition to the alienation of farmers, large parts of the *Mittelstand*, growing numbers of industrialists and of the nationalist right by 1928, there was a further worrying trend facing the regime, the progressive disillusionment of young people and of the literary and cultural elites. The First World War and its aftermath had shaken loose many of the traditional ties binding young people to their families and to their local communities. As the Koblenz authorities noted in the early 1920s, 'the present sad appearance of the young, their debasement on the steeets, in pubs and dance halls results from the absence of firm authority by fathers and by schools during the war. The children of that time are today's young people who have little sense of authority and discipline.' In Cologne, it was observed that young people were spending too much time on 'visits to pubs, excessive drinking and dancing'.

As far as young people themselves were concerned, the early years of Weimar were a liberating experience. There were opportunities to develop leisure interests, to travel to urban centres and to take walking holidays. Out of over 9 million young people in Germany in the 1920s, 4.3 million belonged to a sports club, a church youth organisation or similar body. This covered over 50 per cent of young men, and slightly less than one girl in two. Youth hostelling grew in popularity, as did the cinema and dance halls. The latest American fashions were all the rage, and for the first time young people were able to earn enough to dress distinctively and to move away from home earlier than had hitherto been the case.

Such developments alarmed the older generation, paticularly since they were accompanied by a noticeable rise in juvenile crime and in prostitution. Already in 1917, 27 per cent of all convictions for offences were of 14–18-year-olds, and youth crime continued to account for a sizeable minority of convictions into the 1920s. The other major problem was a steady rise in youth unemployment. Regular jobs were hard to come by after the war, as demobilised soldiers returned to civilian life. Furthermore, because there had been such a big rise in population before 1914, more young people than ever before were looking for work in the 1920s, and the potential work force was swelled by large numbers of young women seeking job opportunities. By 1925, it was estimated that some 200,000 young people under 21 were unemployed; in January 1928, the under-21 age group accounted for 13.4 per cent of the total registered unemployed. The difficulties of finding work in a very competitive and overcrowded labour market undoubtedly had the effect of embittering many young people who were looking to take advantage of the opportunities offered by the new modern age.

As the 1920s progressed, young people also became bored and disillusioned with the political system of the new republic. Political parties were dominated by the prewar generation, who provided the leadership and the candidates. The SPD and the Catholic Centre Party had great difficulty in integrating young members and in accommodating their calls for immediate social change. By 1930, less than 8 per cent of the membership of the SPD were under 25, and fewer than half were under 40. Instead, young people were attracted by the socialist programme of the KPD, or were captivated by the nationalist appeal of parties on the right. By 1928, young people who wished to take an active part in politics were to be increasingly found either in the KPD or in the Nazi Party. Goebbels' contemptuous description of Weimar as an 'old men's republic' struck a chord with growing numbers of young people. They fervently believed that the brave new world which the 1920s had ushered in should consist not of petty political compromises and of deals struck in back rooms but of heroic striving towards national greatness or a socialist society based on strong community values which rose above sectional interests.

Similar sentiments were shared by writers, poets and musicians who flourished in Weimar's liberating environment. While they produced exciting and innovative modes of expression in art, literature, music and architecture, they regarded the republic with considerable contempt. Those on the left felt that the SPD and their Weimar allies had betrayed socialism and crushed all revolutionary

54

aspirations in 1918–19. Since that time so-called progressive parties had been further compromised by coalitions with bourgois nationalist parties. While the democratic system was tolerated by left-wing cultural elites it evoked no strong enthusiasm. On the right, the experimentation and new 'modernism' of Weimar culture aroused fierce criticism and often outrage from traditionalists who associated such 'cultural Bolshevism' with the 'Marxist' government in Berlin. Their fears that the foundations of Germany's strength were being fatally undermined by a decline in morals and in standards of public and artistic life were reinforced by the work of writers such as Spengler. His *Decline of the West* (first published in 1918) painted a gloomy view of the impact of democracy and of capitalism and argued that only a new 'elite of heroes' could save Germany.

The spectre of 'national decline' obsessed writers and artists on the right, and was a fear shared by large numbers of former soldiers and members of nationalist organisations. They believed that the Weimar Republic was hastening Germany's decline as a strong power by promoting political divisions, internationalism and class war. What was required to stop the decay was national unity, a strengthening of authority at the top symbolised by a more powerful President, and an ideology of struggle, discipline and solidarity. For people holding such beliefs, war, far from being a destructive force, had been an exhilarating and uplifting experience which had unified the nation. They felt that some sort of struggle was becoming ever more necessary in order to pull the country out of its lethargy and direct it once more to heroic exploits.

Clearly such views were totally at odds with the existence of a democratic republic. In 1928, they commanded a wide audience and had great appeal for many young people. Nevertheless, the nationalist right was not yet strong enough to end the parliamentary system, though its network of organisations and spokesmen was very successful in using the democratic apparatus to put across its anti-democratic message. The Weimar Republic was still firmly in place in 1928, and it was still able to put together a working coalition, as a result of the election of that year.

But it was becoming clear that the foundation of support on which it rested was becoming significantly weaker. The series of compromises which had brought it into being were beginning to break down. Industrialists were becoming increasingly unwilling to honour the agreements they had reached with workers in 1918–19. The middle classes resented the rising costs and increased taxes of a welfare state. Army leaders feared that the pacifism of the SPD would prevent them from exploiting opportunities for rearmament offered by Germany's improving diplomatic position. And the more national-istic bourgeois parties shared their view that the price of Weimar democracy – weak governments and incessant compromises with the socialist SPD – had become unacceptably high. Significantly, compromises which had seemed so necessary in the turbulent winter of 1918–19 in order to avoid revolution were deemed no longer acceptable now that Germany's economic and international standing had been restored.

It has often been asserted that by 1928, the Weimar Republic was putting down roots and was gaining in acceptability and in support. But the evidence now available suggests that this was not in fact the case, and that strong opposition to the regime was becoming widespread. The very achievements which the republic had recorded in the social and economic sphere were being turned against it in a broad nationalist campaign designed to discredit it and to replace it by a more authoritarian political system. And while the sentiments of those who gave their support to Weimar were often couched in grudging and less than enthusiastic terms, the appeals of the enemies of the republic were fervent, uncompromising and ardently patriotic. Thus even before the full force of the depression hit Germany, the fate of the republic was balanced on a knife-edge, and the odds on the continuation of parliamentary democracy were too close to call.

4

The collapse of Weimar

The onset of the depression, 1928–30

Both inside and outside Germany, the result of the Reichstag election of May 1928, was hailed as a victory for democracy. Appearances, however, were deceptive. The reality was that the recovery by the SPD of its former levels of support, and the success of so many small splinter parties, fuelled the flames of nationalist revolt. There was a greater determination than ever amongst the right wing of the DNVP to mount a challenge to the political system by working closely with right-wing elements in the DVP and with the Nazi Party. This hardening of attitude was symbolised by the election in late 1928 of Alfred Hugenberg as chairman of the DNVP. Hugenburg had been managing director of Krupps steel works before the war, and was now a wealthy press baron, with a string of newspapers and news agencies, as well as interests in film companies across Germany. He was an abrasive and intransigent nationalist, described as 'opinionated and confrontational'. He believed in the exercise of 'dynamic force through principled confrontation' and made it his mission to harry the new government relentlessly, and to organise anti-republican propaganda of an increasingly hysterical kind. As we shall see, his willingness to join forces with other racist and nationalist parties gave Hitler a national platform which he was not slow to exploit.

This change in the attitude of the DNVP had an impact on the

DVP, many of whose members were unwilling to participate in a government alongside members of the SPD. Stresemann did agree to serve in the new cabinet, but only on the basis that it was a 'cabinet of personalities' from various parties who would constitute a grand coalition. On this rather fragile political foundation – of a cabinet not necessarily representing the views or being able to count on the support of its rank-and-file party members – Müller, of the SPD, agreed to form a government. The very broad span of its composition – stretching from the SPD to the DVP and Democrat Party, and embracing the Catholic Centre Party and Bavarian People's Party – made agreement on political issues exceedingly difficult to achieve, particularly from the end of 1928, when the leadership of the Catholic Centre Party passed from Marx to the more right-wing cleric Ludwig Kaas. And as the economic problems facing the new government increased dramatically in scale, more and more deputies withdrew their support and voted against the compromise packages painfully constructed by their party leaders in the cabinet.

What kept the government together until the spring of 1930 was the negotiation of a new reparations agreement under the chairmanship of an American banker, Owen Young. The battle to conclude and to ratify the Young plan, which was devised as a more permanent replacement for the Dawes plan, dominated German politics for over a year. The government held together until the plan had been ratified by the Reichstag and duly signed by Hindenburg, but the force of the nationalist opposition which erupted in the course of 1929 dealt a serious blow not just to Müller's government but to the whole system of parliamentary democracy.

There were three factors which led the government to seek a revision of the Dawes plan by the end of 1928. Under the scheme, German payments had by this time reached their peak of 2,500 million marks per year, and German financial experts were adamant that this sum far exceeded Germany's ability to pay, and needed to be substantially reduced. Political leaders were also keen to remove the external controls on German financial policy and the presence of the reparations agent in Germany. But more important than either of these factors was the French government's insistence that reparations issues had to be definitively settled before it would agree to discuss the early evacuation of the second and third occupation zones in the Rhineland.

Anxious to make progress on the lifting of the Rhineland occupation, the German government accordingly accepted a reparations package negotiated with the allied governments under Young's chairmanship. While it entailed somewhat smaller annual payments over the next few years, and the ending of international controls, the Young plan required Germany to pay a total of 112,000 million marks to the allied governments over a period of nearly sixty years. Such terms were bound to provoke the fury of nationalists throughout Germany, and to serve as a reminder of the hated 'tribute payments' of the Versailles settlement and the 'war guilt lie' on which they rested. Hugenburg was able to use his media empire to protest furiously at what he denounced as the government's weak-kneed acceptance of allied demands and of the proposed enslavement of the children of Germany, and their children in turn, for the next sixty years, as they all laboured under 'the yoke of Young's bondage'.

In the summer of 1929, right-wing racist and nationalist groups came together to set up a 'Reich Committee for a German Referendum' in a bid to challenge the government's acceptance of the Young plan by referring it to the electorate. Taking his place at the table alongside Hugenburg and other right-wing leaders was Adolf Hitler, whose Nazi Party at this stage had only a dozen seats in the Reichstag, and a popular vote of around 800,000. The campaign now unleashed against the Young plan gave Hitler not only a prominent national platform for the first time but also access to many industrial and commercial leaders and their electoral funds. The message which he and his fellow campaigners directed at the German electorate was direct and uncompromising: acceptance of the Young plan entailed acceptance of the war guilt lie. The government should instead be called upon to abrogate article 231, and if ministers and others insisted on ratifying the Young plan, they should be prosecuted for treason and subject to imprisonment or forced labour.

Under the Weimar constitution, 10 per cent of the electorate now had to petition for a referendum on the nationalists' proposals, and for the latter to be considered by the Reichstag. Though 10.02 per cent of voters was secured for the first part of the procedure, the proposals were heavily defeated in the Reichstag in November, and DNVP deputies were divided over the fourth clause demanding prison sentences for those who signed the Young plan. Furthermore, Hindenburg refused to associate himself with the protests, and expressly condemned the fourth clause. A referendum held on 22 December required 21 million votes to bring the proposals into effect; instead it secured only 5.8 million votes. The following March,

despite increasingly desperate attempts by the nationalists to delay the agreement, the Young plan was passed by the Reichstag and signed by Hindenburg 'with a heavy, but also a resolute heart'. There was precious little sympathy for the President, however, in nationalist circles. The German veterans' association, the *Stahlhelm*, solemnly debated whether their honorary member should now be expelled from their ranks, and the Nazi Party newspaper carried headlines proclaiming 'Hindenburg's Farewell to Germany'.

Though the Müller coalition had successfully overcome the furious nationalist challenge to the Young plan, the effort involved had brought the government close to breaking point. In October 1929 Stresemann died, leaving his party to drift to the right. His loss was a great blow to the coalition, and it came at a time when the economic crisis facing the country was beginning to escalate as levels of unemployment climbed relentlessly upwards. Over the winter of 1929–30 it became increasingly difficult for the government to balance the budget and to gain agreement on the taxes to be increased or the economy measures to be introduced. Ironically, it was one of the major welfare achievements of the Weimar Republic, the Unemployment Insurance Act, passed in 1927, which now threatened to engulf the government in a major financial crisis.

The Act provided for modest payments to around 17 million workers if they became unemployed through no fault of their own, had worked for at least fifty-two weeks and had paid a specified number of contributions into the national insurance fund. Both workers and employers were to pay equal contributions of around 3 per cent of the average industrial wage per year. It was estimated that the fund would be able to cover a maximum of 800,000 unemployed workers on average per year – a not unreasonable provision in 1927, when unemployment had fallen to around 4.5 per cent of workers in trade unions. However, over the winter of 1927–8, levels of unemployment rose, putting the scheme under considerable pressure and forcing the government to provide additional funding. By December 1928 unemployment stood at 16.7 per cent and two months later it was at 22.3 per cent, a total of 3 million workers. Again, the government had to step in to provide a loan to keep the scheme afloat. In mid 1929, it was estimated that 1.5 million Germans were drawing on unemployment insurance, and over 10 per cent of the state budget was being consumed by support for the unemployment and social insurance fund.

As a result, employers stepped up their vehement protests against

60

the high taxes which they claimed were necessary to keep the scheme going, and which allegedly prevented them from ploughing profits back into their businesses. Heavy industry in particular singled out high wages and heavy social costs as the root cause of their problems. Hugenberg argued already in 1928 that 'the workers are the only group better off now than in 1913', and that they benefited particularly from compulsory arbitration settlements. As the German economy showed signs of serious contraction, his fellow industrialists demanded an end to 'coercive interference in wage policies, a reduction in intolerable social levies and taxation and a corresponding fiscal reform of the national and municipal governments'. More ominously, many of them subscribed to the view that 'we can only advance in Germany if the parties are in future excluded from negotiations on the formation of governments. So much reform is needed that we cannot think of allowing the parties to have any sort of power in Prussia or the Reich.'

Employers' concerns were increased by the steady worsening of the agrarian situation. Between 1928 and mid-1930, thirteen separate acts were passed in an increasingly desperate bid to protect the grain producers in the east. However, most of the financial assistance went to pay off debts on the larger estates, while owners of small or middling farms saw their narrow profit margins destroyed by a price collapse which became particularly severe after 1928. At the same time, evidence mounted that loans from America were drying up. In the course of 1929, the export of American capital to Germany dropped sharply, from 1,000 million dollars to 200 million, leading to declining share prices on the German stock exchange and to an increased number of bankruptcies. Export markets in Europe and overseas began to disappear behind tariffs hastily erected by anxious governments, and on 24 October 1929 the Wall Street stock market collapsed. As the economic outlook changed from gloomy to distinctly stormy, the financial pressures facing the government grew, placing enormous strains on party unity and on the scope for compromise. As the unemployment insurance fund deficit mounted, the employers' party, the DVP demanded that the level of benefits paid to workers should be cut. Not surprisingly the workers' deputies in the SPD pressed for an increase in contributions. It became more and more difficult for the government to put together a financial package that would secure the agreement of all coalition partners and be sufficient to address the scale of the crisis. On 27 March 1930, Müller resigned. By this stage, a substantial proportion of the electorate, including most of the traditional, administrative and industrial elites, had come to the conclusion that a system of parliamentary democracy could no longer deal effectively with the problems facing the country.

In addition to calls for a move to stronger 'presidential style' government, there was a growing desire amongst the bourgeois parties and the interest groups they represented to exclude the SPD from political power. This objective was fully shared by influential army leaders, in particular the Minister of Defence, Groener, and the head of the army's political office, Kurt von Schleicher. Since the formation of Müller's government, they had worked to ensure that spending on the army and the modernisation of its armaments, much of it conducted in great secrecy, was able to continue without any interference. They were extremely successful – in 1930, Germany was spending 60 per cent more on armaments than in 1913, despite the vastly reduced size of the post-Versailles army. None the less, they resented the need for endless discussions and compromises with the 'pacifist' SPD and strongly supported the prospect of a more presidential-style government. They also favoured moves to reorientate the government coalition further to the right. By the end of the 1920s, army leaders were anxious to exploit the improving international situation, and calculated that if restrictions on the numbers of troops Germany was allowed were to be lifted by negotiations at Geneva, they might need to draw on right-wing para-military formations such as Hitler's SA. Rather than a coalition with the SPD, they believed that the army's interests would be best served by a government which established closer links with patriotic nationalists on the right.

Thus by the end of March 1930, there was a powerful current of opinion in Germany demanding a more authoritarian, anti-Marxist government. Beleaguered by their opponents, and stung by charges of financial incompetence levied in particular by Schacht, the President of the Reichsbank at the end of 1929, the SPD retreated almost thankfully into opposition. Even their closest political allies, the Catholic Centre Party, were by this stage talking about the possibility of government by emergency decree or a dissolution of the Reichstag if the political parties could not reach agreement on measures to tackle the economic and industrial crisis. In the event, the government formed by Müller's replacement, the Reichstag leader of the Centre Party, Brüning, showed little change, other than the absence of SPD members. But it soon became apparent that

Brüning's conception of his role was somewhat different from that of previous Chancellors, and that he was willing to work with Hindenburg to bring about a fundamental shift in power from parliamentary government to a more executive presidential-style government.

Many historians now pinpoint the assumption of power by Brüning as the moment in time when Weimar democracy died. It is obviously easier to come to this conclusion with the benefit of hindsight. At the time, large sections of the German population certainly saw Brüning's 'cabinet of front-line soldiers' as the only possible answer to the crisis facing their country. However, how extensive the support was in 1930 for a permanent replacement of the democratic republic by a more authoritarian regime is more difficult to assess. What is certainly true is that by 1932, after two years of escalating economic crisis and depression on a hitherto unimaginable scale, Weimar democracy was dead in all but name. The only live issue by this stage was what sort of regime would replace it.

Brüning and the great depression, 1930–2

Like its predecessor, Brüning's cabinet was a 'cabinet of personalities', and it faced similar problems of mounting budget deficits and bitter disagreements over how additional revenues could be raised. The political parties were totally unable to reach any sort of compromise over spending cuts or tax increases, and it was therefore impossible for the Minister of Finance to secure Reichstag agreement for his budgetary proposals. He resigned in June 1930, only to see his successor's proposals run into similar difficulties. Despite Brüning's threat to resort to emergency action by invoking article 48, on 16 July the Reichstag voted against a proposal to tax civil servants' earnings by 256 votes to 193. Brüning's response was to use the emergency powers of article 48 to pass the entire finance bill, including the disputed measure, into law.

On 18 July, the SPD moved for a suspension of the emergency decree and they linked this motion with a vote of no confidence. With the support of the Communists, Nazis and a large section of Hugenburg's Nationalists, the motion was passed. At this point, Brüning, stretching the constitution to its limits, dissolved the Reichstag and appealed to the electorate for support for a more authoritarian government in the forthcoming elections. It was a fateful dissolution, which benefited neither the SPD nor Brüning himself. Instead, the great gainer was the bitterest enemy of both sides, the extreme racist and nationalist Nazi Party.

In the first half of 1930, the Nazi Party had been making significant electoral gains in regional elections, in Thuringia, in Baden and then in Saxony. In the Thuringian government, a Nazi member, Frick, was given the office of minister for the interior and for education. The party's popularity amongst university students and amongst junior officers in the Reichswehr was spreading rapidly. Of its 130,000 members in 1930, nearly 70 per cent were under 40 and 37 per cent were under 30. It had expanded its national network through an impressive 1,378 local branches. Yet despite such signals, the surge in support for the Nazi Party in the elections of September, 1930, came as an enormous shock to large numbers of Germans. As Feuchtwanger has noted, 'the Nazi breakthrough was not only sensational, it finally destroyed a party system' which had survived 'the traumatic events of defeat and revolution'. The Nazis increased their vote from 2.6 per cent in 1928 to 18.3 per cent, representing an eight-fold rise in the numbers of voters from 812,000 to 6.4 million. While some Germans contemptuously attributed their startling success to an 'uprising of stupidity', hundreds of thousands of Protestant farmers in northern Germany, craftsmen and small businessmen and their families and unskilled workers in smaller communities, civil servants, women and above all young people responded to the Nazi appeal to turn their backs on the weak parliamentary system, the Treaty of Versailles and the Young plan, and to support a dynamic nationalist party dedicated to the regeneration of Germany.

While the SPD remained the largest single Reichstag party with 143 seats, the Nazis were now the second largest with 107 deputies, who ostentatiously wore their party uniform, with its swastika emblems, and declared their intention of working to abolish all parliamentary institutions. In this objective, they were joined by 77 Communists, who had also seen their party's vote rise by some 2.5 per cent. The Catholic Centre Party's 68 seats was a gain of 7 since 1928, and the Bavarian People's Party also gained a modest 2 to reach 19. Both the DVP and the DNVP lost significant numbers of voters to the Nazis and saw their numbers of deputies decline dramatically, by a third in the case of the DVP and by almost a half in the case of the DNVP.

The situation which Brüning now faced in the Reichstag in the wake of the election was more intractable than ever. The

Communists and Nazis, together totalling about a third of the deputies in the Reichstag, were completely opposed to the Weimar constitution and indeed to any system of parliamentary government.

The weakened nationalist parties, the DVP and DNVP, and the Catholic Centre Party, who had campaigned together to rally electoral support for a 'Hindenburg bloc' so as to relieve them of the necessity of governing with the SPD found themselves in a complete political impasse. They were resolutely opposed to any working arrangement with the largest Reichstag party, the SPD, but the political logic of this was that Brüning was condemned to continuing minority support in the Reichstag, though he could count on the tacit acquiescence in his policies of the SPD. While SPD leaders were not willing to risk further electoral losses to the KPD by giving active support to Brüning's increasingly unpopular economic measures, they now recognised the immense threat posed by the Nazi Party. If they were not able to keep Brüning in office, they feared that his replacement might well be the loud-mouthed, tub-thumping, crude but undeniably charismatic Adolf Hitler.

The impossible situation that he faced in the Reichstag strengthened Brüning's strongly held conviction that only a more authoritarian government was capable of carrying through the unpopular measures necessary to save Germany from economic disaster. The result was that the Reichstag was increasingly by-passed, as Hindenburg used his presidential powers to authorise more and more emergency decrees under article 48 of the constitution. The Reichstag was in session for ninety-four days in 1930, for forty-one days in 1931 and for a mere thirteen days in 1932. While it passed ninety-eight laws in 1930, with only five emergency decrees being authorised, in 1932 it passed only five laws, with a hefty sixty-six emergency decrees deemed necessary. Quite clearly, by 1932 Germany had ceased to operate in any meaningful sense as a parliamentary democracy.

This outcome reflected Brüning's belief that he had no option but to rule by decree, to avoid damaging political compromises and the pressure of vested interest groups. He drew a sharp distinction between the interests of the state, which he saw as being well-served by disciplined and selfless government servants, and 'party political interests' which had made Germany ungovernable in the selfish pursuit of narrow party gain. After the election of 1930, Brüning increasingly relied on the support of the government's administrative machinery and on non-political 'experts' to help him in framing and carrying through his policies. Ministerial positions became administrative appointments above the party political system, and power became concentrated in a small circle of powerful state secretaries. The basis of his political support narrowed considerably, as he bypassed political colleagues and worked through secretive discussions with chosen officials.

In his *Memoirs*, Brüning suggests that he was deliberately aiming to lay the foundations for a return to constitutional monarchy, for a reduction in the federal powers of the regional states, and for a reduced role for directly elected bodies. We do not know the extent to which his objectives were fully formed already in 1930, but there is no doubt that he saw the shift from a parliamentary republic to a more authoritarian regime as not just a temporary measure, to deal with the economic crisis, but as a permanent change. What he had not reckoned with, however, was the progressive demoralisation and radicalisation which his deflationary policies brought about among the German electorate. Their effect was to increase support not for the return of the monarchy or for a reinforced presidential system but for the radical programme put forward by the Nazis.

As well as seeking political and constitutional reforms, Brüning's main objectives were to 'restructure' Germany's economic and financial systems and to end Germany's reparations payments. While he was facing an economic crisis of unprecedented magnitude, there is general agreement that his desire to exploit it to achieve domestic and foreign-policy aims compounded the disastrous situation facing Germany. As the German economy contracted, national income fell sharply, and in 1932 was 39 per cent less in real terms than it had been in 1929. Unemployment spiralled from 3 million to its peak of 6 million registered unemployed in 1932: the real figure of those then out of work, counting temporary female workers and summer labourers, was probably nearer to 9 million, with millions more on reduced hours or fearing the closure of their workshops and factories.

Brüning's reponse was to reduce price and wage levels substantially throughout the German economy, except in the agricultural sector. He was unwavering in his insistence that the crisis could only be overcome by cutting public and welfare expenditure and by imposing the strictest financial discipline on the German people. Reductions in the pensions of wounded war veterans, widows and orphans created great bitterness, as did massive salary cuts and reductions in benefits for unskilled workers and for the lower ranks of the civil service. More senior civil servants saw their income cut by over

20 per cent. At the same time, taxes were increased – there were surcharges on high incomes, taxes on single people and civil servants, a citizens' tax, and increased taxes on tobacco and beer. Even the unpopular turnover tax was increased in the course of 1931, and the level of contributions for unemployment insurance had leapt from 3½ per cent to 6½ per cent. At the same time, Germany's foreign debts had increased from 1 billion Reichsmarks to 3.3 billion.

All these measures contributed to the growing alienation and profound disaffection of the electorate. Unemployed workers who had exhausted their entitlement to state benefits were thrown on to the mercy of their local councils, and had to beg for food and clothing for their families. The single unemployed roamed the streets; large numbers were recruited by the Communist Party and were increasingly involved in street fights with Nazi thugs. Those still in work worried about their future prospects; working women came under strong social pressure to give up their jobs to men whose positions as heads of families cast them, and not their wives or daughters, as the chief bread winners.

Many commentators, at the time and since, have argued that there were alternatives to Brüning's deflationary policies, that measures could have been introduced to stimulate credit formation and to create comprehensive job-creation programmes. But such alternatives would have undermined Brüning's main objectives, to use the crisis to end Germany's reparation payments, to dismantle Weimar's comprehensive and elaborate system of welfare provisions and to reduce Germany's manufacturing costs in order to make her industry more competitive than that of her European neighbours.

Throughout 1930 and 1931, Brüning's policy was aimed at persuading the allies that Germany could no longer afford to make reparation payments. He told a meeting of the Centre Party's Reichstag group in August 1931, that 'only deflation could convince the world that Germany could not afford to pay reparations'. Any sign of economic recovery would undermine Germany's campaign to secure allied recognition of her near-bankruptcy. In June 1931, President Hoover of the United States did indeed agree to a moratorium on reparations payments. But by this time, the failure of the *Kreditanstalt*, the largest bank in Austria, following on from a disastrously ill-judged proposal from the Austrian and German governments for a customs union in March 1931, had triggered off a banking crisis in Germany itself. Within days of an agreement being reached with France over the moratorium, Germany's largest bank, the Danatbank, collapsed. Another bank, the Dresdener, was also in difficulties, as more and more local authorities and municipal councils faced insolvency.

In the face of such unprecedented financial disasters, trade unions had no hope of holding on to their hard-won rights and welfare provisions. Every downward spiral in the prevailing economic situation was utilised by Brüning to force down costs and wages in a vain endeavour to drive Germany through the crisis and to enable her to emerge in a stronger and more competitive position, while her erstwhile enemies were still engulfed in depression. He told Hitler at one of their first meetings in 1930 that 'the first country to implement all the unpopular domestic measures necessary will rise to the top'. Thus Brüning shared with the Nazis a desire to use the crisis to bring an end to the Versailles shackles and to restore Germany to a position of political and economic dominance in Europe. But while he worked to bring about revision under the leadership of the traditional German elites – the army, large landowners, and senior government officials, and to pave the way for the restoration of the monarchy, the Nazis worked to harness the misery and despair of the German masses for a far more radical political programme.

As Nazi support in local elections increased dramatically in the course of 1931, Brüning found his own position challenged by increasing hostility from industrialists, from the army, and from large landowners in the east. In October 1931 there was a great anti-Marxist rally of right-wing national opposition groups at Bad Harzburg, masterminded by Hugenberg. The Nazis used the occasion to demonstrate the strength of their support and to pose as dedicated, if impatient, patriots. Hitler had already emphasised his intention to work against the republic by legitimate means rather than through violence at a trial of three army officers the previous year, thereby enhancing his nationalist appeal and political legitimacy. In January 1932, Groener told fellow army leaders that Hitler was a 'modest, decent individual, with best intentions. In appearance the keen, self-taught type. . . . Intentions and aims of Hitler are good, but he is an enthusiast, ardent, diffuse. . . . The Nazis have to be justly treated, only excesses to be fought not the movement as such.'

Meanwhile, Schacht, no longer at the head of the Reichsbank but still a very influential financier, threw his weight behind the nationalist opposition and against Brüning, referring to the mark as 'a currency which no longer serves the normal exchange of goods, but has the sole purpose of hiding the illiquidity of our financial institutions and of the public purse'. In the army, von Schleicher was weighing up the possibilities of broadening the government by bringing in the Nazis, in an effort to 'tame them', and effecting a transition to a permanent authoritarian regime based on a strong President and backed by the army. However, the first meeting in October 1931 between Hindenburg and Hitler, who was accompanied by Goering, did not go well. The 84-year-old Field Marshall took an instant dislike to Hitler, regarding him as an uneducated social upstart and referring to him afterwards with contempt as the 'Bohemian corporal'.

Hindenburg's patience with Brüning was also reaching its limits by 1932. There were several reasons for the old man's disillusionment with his former protégé. In the first place, Brüning's economic cuts had alienated and driven into opposition not just socialist-inclined workers and their families, but respectable and well-connected civil servants and government officials. Secondly, Hindenburg's son Oskar and his military and aristocratic confidants were increasingly attracted by the radical programme of national reconstruction put forward by the Nazis, just as they were strongly opposed to Brüning's support for a ban on the public activities of the Nazi SA and SS. This ban was finally agreed to extremely reluctantly by Hindenburg in April 1932, despite the Crown Prince's protest against the disbanding of 'this magnificent body of men', but caused great anger in military circles. Thirdly, Brüning had failed to extend the President's term of office, due to expire in early 1932, by parliamentary means, and Hindenburg found himself facing the disagreeable prospect of a presidential election.

Nothing highlights the change which had taken place in the German political landscape since the late 1920s more vividly than this election campaign. Hindenburg found it exceedingly difficult to secure the support of right-wing nationalist parties. The veterans' organisation, the *Stahlhelm*, and Hugenberg's Nationalists refused to support him. When the former emperor forbade his son, the Crown Prince, to stand as a candidate, Goebbels announced that Hitler would stand. Even in the *Junker* heartlands of East Prussia, strong support was forthcoming for the 'Bohemian corporal'. The majority of the East Prussian Chamber of Agriculture requested Hindenburg to resign in favour of Hitler! Hindenburg was put in the humiliating position of having to woo the despised Socialists and the Catholic Centre Party, while Hitler was the favoured candidate of the nationalist parties. In the first ballot, on 13 March 1932, Hindenburg secured over 18.5 million votes as against Hitler's 11.3 million, but narrowly failed to win an overall majority. He was thus forced to a second round, and though he won fairly comfortably, Hitler still received an extremely respectable vote of almost 37 per cent.

The final straw for Brüning came with landed opposition to a state scheme designed to broaden the 'Eastern Relief' programme. While great landowners had to some extent escaped the drastic economies imposed on the rest of the population and had required generous state subsidies and tariff protection, special treatment had not been sufficient to save all estates from bankruptcy. However, plans whereby the state would acquire some of this land, by compulsory purchase if necessary, and resettle landless labourers on it, aroused the deep anger of Prussian *Junkers*. They expressed their total opposition to such 'agrarian Bolshevism' to their fellow estate-owner, Hindenburg, in very explicit terms. Indeed, the Director of the East Prussian Agricultural Society warned of the dire effects such measures would have on men who had 'hitherto been the bearers of the national will to resist Poland by force of arms'.

As a result of all these factors, Hindenburg felt that he could no longer keep Brüning in office. With the decline in influence of the Reichstag, and government now proceeding by means of a series of emergency decrees, Brüning could stay in power only if Hindenburg remained willing to continue granting the decrees. By the end of May 1932, he was no longer prepared to do so. A month before the final cancellation of all reparations payments was declared at Lausanne, Brüning's cabinet resigned, on 30 May 1932. As he later expressed it, he fell '100 metres from his goal'. It was left to others to reap the benefits of all his efforts.

Presidential rule to Nazi rule: June 1932–January 1933

Brüning was replaced as Chancellor by a man few Germans had heard of, Franz von Papen. Though he was a member of the Catholic Centre Party, his political experience had been largely confined to the Prussian *Landtag*. Far from being a typical Weimar deputy, he was a wealthy aristocrat and retired cavalry major who believed that government should revert to being the preserve of gentlemen, reserve officers, barons and great landowners. His cabinet therefore did not contain a single member of the middle class, let alone a working man, and none of its members was a Reichstag deputy. All ministers ostentatiously renounced their party memberships on taking office to emphasise that their appointments transcended party politics and that their power derived from the President and from the state, not from the people. Von Papen's elevation owed much to the recommendation of his former General Staff classmate, Kurt von Schleicher, and both Hindenburg and von Schleicher hoped that Hitler and the Nazi Party could be prevailed upon to support him, without the need for an incessant stream of emergency decrees.

One of von Papen's first measures was to lift the ban on the SA and the SS. This was followed by a bold measure to remove the local and regional powers of the state of Prussia, an area in which the SPD had exercised strong political influence, and to place the state directly under the control of a Reich Commissioner. The move was allegedly aimed against the threat of a communist uprising which the state government had not taken any action to suppress. Despite the far-reaching political implications of the move, 'not a hand was raised . . . to defend the strongest surviving stronghold of the Republic'. With widespread unemployment continuing, and the struggle to exist from day to day consuming the attention of the population – even of trade union and SPD activists – no-one had the stomach for a political confrontation, and a run-in with Nazi opponents. Thus another bastion of Weimar democracy had fallen.

Flushed with triumph, von Papen confidently awaited the results of fresh elections, which had been declared for the end of July. But it was already clear from huge increases in support for Hitler and the Nazi Party in state elections, that once again Hitler would be the principal beneficiary of the never-ending economic crisis. With nearly 6 million workers now officially registered as out of work, the Nazi vote rocketed once again, with support from nearly 14 million Germans, resulting in an increase from 110 seats to 230. The Communists also increased their seats, from 78 to 89. While the SPD experienced slight losses, and the Catholic Centre Party made modest gains, the liberal and conservative parties suffered severely, retaining only 22 of their previous 122 seats. Even Hugenberg's Nationalists lost 5 seats. With 37 per cent of the vote, the Nazis had gained support across the political spectrum, but particularly from the other nationalist parties and special interest and single-issue parties.

With their modern campaigning slogans and strong nationalist image, the impact of the Nazis on the electorate, and particularly the charismatic appeal of Hitler, was undeniable. With 319 seats out of a total of 608, the Nazis and Communists now commanded an absolute majority in the Reichstag. Surely it would only be a matter of time before Hitler and some of his fellow Nazis took office in a new government.

The negotiations and 'backstairs intrigues' which now began revolved not around whether or not Hitler should be given a government post – this could hardly be denied him, given the size of the Nazi vote – but around the terms on which he should be brought into power. Von Papen was willing to agree to Hitler's becoming Vice-Chancellor in his government, and to allow his fellow Nazis a number of ministerial posts, but no more. Von Schleicher, however, thought that Hitler's strong showing in the election justified his appointment as Chancellor, and tried to bring Hindenburg round to this point of view. The President remained obdurately unimpressed with Hitler, and when Hitler told him at a meeting on 13 August that he would not co-operate with the new government unless appointed as Chancellor, the President responded that he could not accept that responsibility 'before God, his conscience and the Fatherland'.

However, Hitler had many ways in which he could continue to press his claims. If Hindenburg would not let him become Chancellor, then he could work to construct a majority coalition in the Reichstag. To this end, he entered into negotiations with the Catholic Centre and Bavarian People's parties. An alliance between 'the black' (the clerical Catholic Centre Party) and 'the brown' (Nazi Party) had already operated successfully in some regional parliaments, on a common programme of anti-Marxism. Now Hitler sought to use it to further his ambitions to gain the Chancellorship. Von Papen could not allow the Reichstag to be mobilised against him in this way, as a 'black and brown' coalition could easily vote him out of power. Both Hindenburg and von Papen regarded this assertion of Reichstag power as an affront to Presidential power, and as a consequence von Papen was given the authorisation to dissolve the Reichstag and to call fresh elections. The Reichstag's response was to pass a vote of 'no confidence' in von Papen's government by the overwhelming margin of 512 votes to 42, but attempts to argue against such an early dissolution on the grounds that it was unconstitutional were nevertheless unsuccessful.

The second Reichstag election of 1932 was held on 6 November and in the intervening period from mid September von Papen's government tried to alleviate economic distress by a programme which included measures designed to create new jobs, as well as proposals to simplify the social services and further cut costs. The Voluntary Labour Service, which the government introduced, provided the foundation for more ambitious schemes to put unemployed people back to work introduced by the Nazis the following year. To appease the agricultural lobby, von Papen's government granted a land tax remission of 40 per cent, banned the auctioning of defaulted estates and instituted quotas on dairy and livestock imports.

By the time of the election, the economic crisis had certainly passed its peak, though voters were still suffering from the consequences. Furthermore, political parties, and in particular the Nazi Party, had expended a considerable part of their funds on the earlier election campaign, and now had to cut back somewhat on their electioneering. None the less, the Nazi Party remained popular, with 11.7 million voters supporting it, as against 13.7 million in July, and a total of 196 seats. There was an increase in support for the Nationalists, from 14 to 51 seats, and modest losses for the Catholic Centre and the Bavarian People's Party. But on the left, the clear gainers were the German Communists, whose number of seats rose from 89 seats to 100. They were now almost as strong as the SPD, whose support had fallen, and who now held only 121 seats.

Commentators at the time and since have made much of the fact that the Nazi Party had suffered a serious setback, receiving the support of only 33 per cent of the electorate, as against over 37 per cent in July. Is this a clear sign that their support had peaked and that they were now declining rapidly as a as a political force? If this was a possibility, it was one which worried many Catholic Centre and right-wing leaders as they witnessed the continuing rise of the 'Bolshevik peril'. Around one-sixth of the electorate had supported the Communist Party, whose vote was heavily concentrated in the major industrial areas and in Berlin. To counter this subversive political force, party leaders from the Centre Party across to the right of the political spectrum were agreed that Hitler had to be given a prominent role in any new government. But the difficulty lay in agreeing on what that role should be. Was it finally to be the Chancellorship, or would Hitler now accept something less?

In prolonged negotiations with von Papen and then with Hindenburg, Hitler stuck to his insistence on the Chancellorship or nothing. He justified this stance by arguing that if Nazism as a movement collapsed 'then Germany will be in the greatest danger, then there will be 18 million Marxists and among them perhaps 14 or 15 million Communists. It is therefore entirely in the national interest that my movement should survive and this presupposes that my movement will have the lead.' Still von Papen and Hindenburg refused to accede to Hitler's demand. But increasing numbers of important interest groups – amongst industrialists, in the army, even in Hindenburg's own family circle – were arguing that Hitler should be brought in to power at the head of a new government, and that there was no other way to break the deadlock with the Reichstag and to combat the menace of Communism. The Chairman of the Catholic Centre Party, Kaas, told Hindenburg in late November 1932, 'There are 12 million Germans in the right opposition (Nazi Party) and 13.5 in the left (KPD 6 million, SPD 7.3 million) with the communists growing stronger daily. The left could unify at any time and it is going to be a long, cold winter. The NSDAP must be brought . . . into government now.'

Von Papen instead toyed with the idea of a 'New State', a state without political parties, trade unions or a popularly elected Reichstag but with an authoritarian style of government backed by the army and police. But at a cabinet meeting on 2 December, von Papen could find few backers for such a prospect, particularly when army representatives demurred at the challenge of trying to keep order in the streets against mass demonstrations of Nazis and Communists, while at the same time defending the country's frontiers. Von Papen, accordingly, offered his resignation, and von Schleicher now came out of the shadows to see if he as the new Chancellor could strike a deal with the Nazis.

Von Schleicher's strategy rested on two main aims: to try to negotiate with a more amenable Nazi leader than Hitler, thus splitting the Nazi Party, and to solicit the support of workers and their unions by repealing some of von Papen's more reactionary economic measures. He failed comprehensively on both counts. His attempts to bring the Nazis into government under Gregor Strasser as his Vice-Chancellor came to an abrupt end as Strasser pulled out of negotiations, resigned all his party posts, and took off for an Italian holiday. Hitler had managed to hold the Nazi Party firm and united behind his own uncompromising political demands despite considerable unrest at the failure to secure tangible rewards for their recent electoral successes. Von Schleicher's negotiations with union leaders were no more successful, as the SPD condemned his advances and pressed for contacts to be broken off.

Von Schleicher's attempt to break the political stalemate by making overtures to the unions was roundly condemned in nationalist and presidential circles and by leading industrialists. As Hugenburg graphically observed, 'Schleicher is wooing and messing around with the rotten Red Masses. His cabinet only appears presidential; in truth he is making himself dependent on parties.' The hapless new Chancellor had succeeded only in arousing against him the united opposition of employers and powerful rural interests, who feared that he was reviving some of Brüning's policies. And, perhaps even more significantly, he had incurred the wrath of von Papen.

By early January 1933, it had become very clear that neither von Schleicher nor von Papen could form an effective government, which took some account of popular feelings, without Hitler. It seemed that all possible alternative avenues had been explored, with a singular lack of success. Therefore it became a contest between the two leaders as to which would be the first to strike a deal with Hitler which he would be willing to accept. With von Schleicher unable to muster support in the Reichstag, and Hindenburg unwilling to contemplate yet another dissolution, the way was clear for von Papen to try to construct a 'government of national concentration' with Hitler at its head. The main obstacle to this was the President himself, who still remained unwilling to see Hitler appointed to the office of Chancellor. But in a series of further negotiations with von Papen, which by 22 January were involving the President's son Oskar, Hitler was extremely modest in his political demands, seeking only a few ministerial posts for fellow Nazis apart from his own appointment as Chancellor. At the same time, von Schleicher's attempts to win support from Nationalists and from other Reichstag parties had come to nothing, and he resigned on 28 January. Now von Papen and Oskar von Hindenburg stepped up their attempts to persuade the President that Hitler could do little damage as Chancellor of a nationalist government, with von Papen as his Vice-Chancellor. He would be 'framed in' by respectable nationalists; indeed, within two months, he would be 'squeezed . . . into a corner until he squeaks'. Meanwhile, the new government would have the support of the Reichstag and of the public at large, it would work with Hitler to change the political constitution by passing an enabling act, and then in due course it could dispense with Hitler's services.

Hindenburg proved to be a more astute political judge of character than those around him. He did not share von Papen's extremely optimistic prediction of the future course of events but by the end of January 1933 he accepted that he had run out of alternative options. He finally agreed to appoint Hitler as Chancellor, and to grant him the measure which he had refused to von Schleicher, a dissolution of the Reichstag should it prove to be necessary. And within an exceedingly short space of time, von Papen's vision of the future had evaporated, Hindenburg's fears had proved to be well-founded, and the Weimar Republic had been brutally replaced by the Third Reich.

5

Weimar in retrospect

Books and articles on the Weimar Republic have inevitably been coloured by the atrocities of the Nazi regime which replaced it. Weimar democracy patently failed to prevent Hitler from coming to power and establishing a Nazi dictatorship, and thus for the most part studies have been concerned with identifying the reasons for this failure. Different factors have been singled out for blame: the mistaken tactics of the German Communist Party or of the Social Democrats, the enduring strength of traditional social and economic elites, backstairs intrigue in the crucial winter months of 1932–3 or the failure to establish a strong foundation for democracy at the outset. There has been an ongoing and vigorous debate on all these alleged weaknesses of Weimar democracy, but in recent years historians have also attempted to look at Weimar Germany from a longer-term perspective, as a crucial stage in the complex evolution over the past 100 years of a modern and highly industrialised central European state.

This final chapter will focus on a number of major themes which have been at the centre of historical debate since the second world war. Was the regime really 'doomed from the outset' as many historians have argued, or was its eventual failure based rather on the escalating crises of the late 1920s and in particular the impact of the depression? To help us to arrive at a considered overall conclusion, we need to take account of the limited nature of the German revolution and the problems facing those political parties who were faced with the task of making the new republic work effectively. The chapter will consider the role played by traditional elites and by powerful industrialists, and also briefly examine the problems posed by the faltering German economy throughout the 1920s. It will consider the degree of support which the regime enjoyed by the late 1920s, and assess the extent to which the regime was betrayed after 1930. It will conclude that the crucial weakness of the Weimar Republic lay not in the strength of its enemies but in the striking absence of its friends. For most of its life, the regime was not able to mobilise more than grudging support from large sections of the German electorate. In the last resort, the regime lacked legitimacy. As crisis succeeded crisis, the ability of a democratic regime to deliver strong and effective policies in the circumstances of the later 1920s came into serious question, and other political options promised greater success. Rather than allocate blame for this development amongst a possible range of culprits, historians writing in recent years have rather stressed the profound changes taking place in Germany after the First World War, and the impact of the war and of defeat on a deeply divided but rapidly modernising society.

The main theme of nearly all studies of the Weimar Republic has been failure. Historians have stressed its weakness and instability, describing it variously as an 'improvised democracy', an 'emergency solution', a 'makeshift' republic. It was 'doomed from the outset' by the circumstances of its birth or 'a gamble' which stood 'virtually no chance of success'. In his classic study *Weimar Culture: The Outsider as Insider*, Peter Gay observed that the Weimar Republic was 'born in defeat, lived in turmoil and died in disaster'.

There is general agreement that the regime could not have been established in more inauspicious circumstances, in a defeated country at the end of a long and gruelling war. But a further important issue to consider is the extent to which the German people actually supported the introduction of a democratic republic in late 1918. The German historian Wilhelm Mommsen conceded in 1928 that 'the German republic was not the result of a great republican movement and of republican aspirations of broad circles of our people but it arose as the only possible form for the new state after the collapse at the end of the World War'. And his son Hans argued sixty years later that from 1919 onwards, 'the silent majority regarded democracy as an imported product implanted in Germany under allied pressure in 1919'. Helmut Heiber, in his book *The Weimar Republic*, agreed that while many people in Germany in 1918 wanted an extension of democracy, they envisaged this as resulting from a progressive reform of the existing system of constitutional monarchy established in 1870. The imposition of a democratic republic on Germany by her enemies was bound to arouse wide resentment and to discredit the new regime from the outset. Futhermore the removal of the Kaiser, insisted upon by President Wilson as a pre-condition for the signing of the Armistice, antagonised large sections of the population and left a serious vacuum in the German political structure, which was only partially filled after 1925 by the election to the Presidency of Field Marshall Hindenburg.

Viewed from this perspective, the achievements of the German revolution could be argued to be quite far-reaching and not as narrowly based as some historians have alleged. A very ambitious republican constitution, giving voting rights to men and women of 20 and over, was accompanied by a declaration of wide-ranging social and economic rights. The labour movement secured the recognition of trade unions, negotiating powers and representative councils within larger workshops and factories, and most crucially an eight-hour working day. However, historians are right to emphasise that influential sections of the German population after 1918 saw free trade unions and left-wing parties such as the SPD as 'fundamentally illegitimate', enjoying political power only as a result of the revolutionary disturbances of 1918–19. Leading industrialists could not adjust to the idea of treating trade unions as equal bargaining partners; traditional elites did not regard the new republic as a legitimate successor to the prewar imperial regime.

It is in this respect that the revolution has been viewed as being crucially restricted. Many historians, such as Eberhard Kolb and Rürup have argued that what was required at this point in time was a social revolution to wrest power and influence from the traditional elites in Germany and to lay firm foundations for the new republic. As David Abraham illustrated so clearly in *The Collapse of the Weimar Republic*, without far-reaching social and economic changes, the new democratic regime could not operate effectively. Controversy has raged over whether such changes were possible, the extent to which the SPD leadership 'sold out' to the forces of conservatism to foil the ambitions of the radical left, and the potential for change of the *Räte* or council movement.

There is no doubt that a bitter struggle for political influence was being waged in late 1918 between the radical socialists who were looking to fan the flames of revolution across Germany and the moderate socialists who were pursuing a more limited set of political and economic goals. Radical critics at the time accused Ebert and his SPD colleagues of betraying the interests of workers and of ensuring the failure of the republic by allying with the army and with government officials to crush socialism. More recently, historians such as Kolb have criticised the SPD for their political naivety, for their limited political vision and for their failure to work with revolutionary councils to secure significant economic and social changes in the ownership of wealth and property.

However, in recent years, historians such as Mommsen and Peukart have questioned how much support there was amongst the German population for fundamental change in 1918. They have drawn attention instead to the fear which large sections of the population had of 'Russian solutions' being forced upon them, and of continuing chaos and disorder. While the opportunity to extend the political influence of workers' and soldiers' councils might well have existed, it is equally possible to argue that such an attempt might have resulted in civil war. There can be no doubt that one of the strongest factors influencing Ebert in November 1918 was his desire to stave off further social and political unrest, to end the war and to bring home the German army without Germany's enemies being able to capitalise further on her manifestly weak position. Above all else, Ebert was a German patriot, who was not prepared to risk the invasion or dismemberment of the country in the pursuit of far-reaching revolutionary goals.

According to some historians, Ebert's prudence and moderation inevitably doomed the new republic to political failure. Without fundamental social and economic changes, they argue, and the extensive democratisation of the German people, the new republic could never wield effective political power in the face of the continuing hostility of the entrenched traditional elites such as the *Junkers*, senior government officals and army officers. Others, however, believe that there was not sufficient popular support for an extensive programme of change, involving the break-up of large landed estates or the nationalisation of heavy industry. Ebert successfully pursued limited constitutional and economic goals, while at the same time ensuring that Germany retained her unity and most of her territory.

There is no doubt that the most damaging legacy of the German revolution was the rift which opened up on the left between the revolutionary socialists and the more moderate SPD. The brutal suppression of workers' uprisings in the early years of the republic was neither forgotten nor forgiven by the German Communist Party, and fierce rivalries continued to undermine the political stability of the new republic as the two main left-wing parties competed for working-class support. Between them the two parties gained the support of 30–40 per cent of the Weimar electorate, but their total inability to work together constructively undoubtedly contributed to the failure of the democratic regime. Some historians have emphasised the intransigence and unrealistic political agenda of the German Communist Party, particularly in the face of the growing Nazi threat, while others have criticised the political tactics of the SPD. But discussion has also focused more generally on the inability of those parties who supported the regime to broaden the basis of their popular support.

Whilst there were effective coalitions at regional level between the Catholic Centre Party, the SPD and the Democrats, Weimar parties remained fairly narrowly based, on a class, religious or regional basis. The SPD saw itself as a workers' party, existing to advance the economic and social interests of the working class, and joining government coalitions only reluctantly in order to safeguard those interests. All attempts to transform itself into a more broadly based party of the left and centre failed. Instead, in the late 1920s it retreated into 'traditional policies of class isolation', trying vainly to defend its members against the worst effects of the depression. The Catholic Centre Party had a broader base of support amongst different social classes than the SPD but its appeal was limited by its religious affiliation which was espoused by a minority of the German population, heavily concentrated in the south and east of the country.

Individual political parties have been criticised for their failure to make Weimar democracy work. However, in recent years historians have drawn attention to the abrupt transformation of the political landscape which took place in Germany at the end of the war. Parties which before 1914 had been driven underground and excluded from power were suddenly given the task of ending the war, supervising the disbanding of the army and creating social and economic order. Not surprisingly, they struggled to make the transition from impotent opposition to effective government. They found it difficult to operate on a broad national basis, to work with other parties or to develop manifestoes which were inclusive rather than exclusive. Ironically, the party which was most successful in generating mass support across class, religious and regional divides was the Nazi Party. The reasons for its wide popular appeal have been debated at enormous length, most notably in a recent comprehensive study by Thomas Childers, *The Nazi Voter*. What is clear is that the mass support which Hitler was able to mobilise was a major factor in his rise to power, and it was broad-based support across the political and social spectrum which other parties had been unable to generate.

Another political weakness in the Weimar Republic which historians have highlighted is the decline of German liberalism. Indeed, Peukart has singled out the decline of bourgeois liberalism and specifically of the Democrat Party and of the German People's Party as the 'decisive event' of Weimar politics, which undermined the pro-republic centre 'from within'. The long-term decline of German liberalism, accelerated by the collapse of middle-class confidence in the regime in the 1920s, resulted in the fragmentation of bourgeois parties, which made it possible for the Nazis to exploit the political weakness of the regime and to capitalise on the growing economic tensions. The historian Larry Eugene Jones has made a particular study of the dissolution of the bourgeois party system, emphasising the fact that bourgeois splinter parties in the 1928 Reichstag elections gained nearly 12 per cent of the popular vote, and that a quarter of the votes cast in that election went to parties who gained less than 5 per cent of the total vote. Thus while working-class support was mainly split between the two parties of the left, middle-class support was fragmented to a much greater degree. Patently, Weimar lacked firm political foundations and a common set of political goals, apart from a univeral desire to overturn the Versailles settlement.

Increasingly, historians have drawn attention to the enormous economic problems which were inherited by the new republic and which inexorably sapped its strength. Richard Bessel has highlighted the economic, social and psychological impact of the war, and the extent to which Germany was impoverished after the war. Only the most drastic government economies and massive tax increases would have begun to address Germany's economic problems, and no government was willing to court the electoral unpopularity which such measures would inevitably have aroused, especially after the outcry which greeted Erzberger's early attempts at tax reforms. The alternative was to let the mark depreciate, and this policy was continued to its fateful conclusion in 1923, when the Ruhr invasion triggered hyper-inflation. It is true that the republic survived this massive crisis, but one consequence was the loss of a significant amount of middle-class political support. Those people who saw their hard-earned savings or rents lose all value while at the same time

82

those with significant debts appeared to benefit from the crisis were left feeling extremely bitter. They were further antagonised by the lengthy haggling which accompanied the government's revaluation of assets and debts in 1924. Many middle-class families thus blamed the regime for the loss of their wealth and assets, leaving it severely weakened, and in no position to weather the further economic storms which beset it in the late 1920s.

Harold James has argued that 'Germany's economic crisis preceded both the world depression and the political collapse. Weimar's economy suffered from an inherent instability.' He has itemised Weimar's economic problems under seven heads: 'world economic conditions, unfavourable demographic developments, low savings and investment rates, misinvestment, falling profitability, instability of public finance and excessive protection of industry'. Other historians have focused on individual economic issues. The causes of falling profitability in particular have aroused extensive debate, being blamed by some on excessive wage awards to workers outstripping productivity gains, and by others on lack of investment by employers.

What is clear, however, is that the absence of any real economic growth in Germany in the 1920s had profound political consequences. Political parties in government had no room for manoeuvre and no scope for political or economic 'trade-offs'. Instead of being able to mobilise support by distributing economic gains, they were forced to preside over painful cuts in living standards. It was this chill economic climate rather than political parties' inability to operate the democratic Weimar machinery, according to Peukart, which was responsible for ineffective political coalitions and the steady loss of electoral support. As he argues, the republic was based on a series of social and economic compromises, all of which broke down in the later 1920s. Given the scale of the economic problems, the existing divisions in German society and the pressures of a modernising state, the new republic was unable to generate the confidence necessary to guarantee its survival.

Dick Geary has emphasised the enduring tensions between workers and employers, and the growing reluctance of industrialists to accept such features of the new regime as arbitration awards, the eight-hour working day and the costs of the unemployment insurance scheme. The Weimar Republic aroused contempt from traditional elites such as the *Junkers* on the one hand, but perhaps equally significantly failed to enlist the support of the modernisers in German society, the industrial magnates, who were busy re-equipping their factories after 1924 with American loans, and the army officers seeking to harness the military potential of advancing technology. Such groups, by the late 1920s, had lost confidence in the capacity of a democratic regime to stabilise and to regenerate Germany. The debate centred instead on what sort of regime should take its place.

It is clear that the historical discussion about the reasons for the failure of Weimar democracy has become a very broad-ranging one. Historians have focused on a variety of political and economic issues, and have carried out extensive analyses of the extent of social and demographic change taking place in Germany in the first two decades of the twentieth century. There is now a far more sympathetic understanding of the problems facing German leaders in the 1920s, and the difficulties they encountered in trying to deal with them. Rather than apportioning blame, historians now seek to explain the great tensions and enduring divisions which made the achievement of political stability so difficult, and to give credit to the advances which were made. Given the circumstances of its birth, and the succession of crises it faced, it is clear that the regime was already facing a serious loss of confidence on the part of significant numbers of voters by 1928. Once the full force of the depression hit Germany, the prospects for its survival were far from good.

It is ironic that while the democratic system itself became discredited, the radicalised mass electorate which remained in being switched its support to anti-democratic extremist parties of the left and the racist-nationalist right. While it is not technically correct to argue that Hitler was 'voted into power', there is no doubt that the support of over a third of the German electorate gave Hitler and his Nazi colleagues an enormously strong bargaining position. While there was a considerable amount of political intrigue taking place in Presidential circles by late 1932, it was by no means clear what alternatives to a Hitler-led government existed at that stage which could muster a broad base of popular support. It was comparatively easy to demolish the fragile Weimar regime, but far more difficult to construct a strong alternative which would enjoy popular backing. Again, the passage of time has enabled historians to look more dispassionately at the events which led to Hitler's accession to power in 1933, and to shift discussion from apportioning blame to acknowledging the complex of reasons why Hindenburg and von Papen acted in the way they did.

It is only in recent years that historians have been able to assess

Germany's first involvement in democracy from a longer-term perspective and to compare it with the evolution of the West German state after 1945. Looked at over a more extensive time-scale, the achievements of the Weimar Republic can be more clearly balanced against its failures, and both can be compared instructively with more recent developments in West Germany. Viewed in this way, the Weimar Republic can be seen as representing the first tentative steps towards the establishment of a modern, unitary, democratic state. At national, regional and local levels, men and women from all social classes were encouraged to participate actively in the political system. Welfare schemes were greatly expanded, and both sexes, young and old, could enjoy a wide range of sporting, social and cultural activities. Tragically, this period of advance was followed by a convulsive lurch backwards, but the roots of this dramatic reversal can now be traced back not just to 1929 or to 1918, but to the decades before 1914. Weimar Germany was a society in transition, a society that was experiencing the pressures of modernisation and of industrialisation. The newly established democratic structure was not strong enough to cope effectively with such underlying pressures when they were reinforced by new social and economic tensions arising from war and from defeat. The collapse of the regime gave Hitler his opportunity to try to create a new racial order in Germany and in Europe, and millions perished as a consequence. But we owe it to those countless victims not just to apportion blame for failure and for what followed to individual actors or to particular groups in Weimar Germany, but to dig deeper and to try to uncover the full range of obstacles which combined to derail Germany's first attempt at democracy.

Further reading

General reading

E. J. Feuchtwanger, *From Weimar to Hitler: Germany 1918–33* (Macmillan, 1993). A detailed and very balanced assessment of the problems faced by the new republic.

H. Heiber, *The Weimar Republic* (Blackwell, 1993). Good general account of events, though first published in 1966.

I. Kershaw (ed.), *Weimar: Why did German Democracy Fail?* (Weidenfeld, 1990). Introduction by Kershaw followed by a stimulating debate between four leading historians on the problems of Weimar.

J. Kocka, *Facing Total War: German Society 1914–18* (Berg, 1984).

E. Kolb, *The Weimar Republic* (Unwin Hyman, 1988).

A. J. Nicholls, *Weimar and the Rise of Hitler* (Macmillan, 1968). Classic account of the rise of Nazism, though now a little dated.

J. Noakes and G. Pridham (ed.), *Nazism, 1919–45, A Documentary Reader, vol. 1: The Rise to Power* (Exeter University Press, 1983). A comprehensive and clearly structured collection of primary sources with helpful analysis of context.

D. Peukart, *The Weimar Republic* (Penguin, 1991). One of the most recent and stimulating accounts of the Weimar republic, setting it with Germany's longer-term development as a modern state.

More specialised studies

D. Abraham, *The Collapse of the Weimar Republic* (Princeton University Press, USA, 1981).

R. Bessell, *Germany after the First World War* (Clarendon Press, 1993). Contains a wealth of social and economic material on the impact of the First World War on Germany.

R. Bessell and E. Feuchtwanger (ed.), *Social Change and Political Development in Weimar* (Croom Helm, 1981). A collection of detailed but interesting essays.

T. Childers, *The Nazi Voter* (University of North Carolina Press, USA, 1983). A detailed discussion of the social and economic roots of Nazi support.

P. Gay, *Weimar Culture* (Penguin, 1969). Classic study of the relationship between writers, artists and intellectuals and the new republic.

J. Hiden, *Germany and Europe 1919–39* (Longman, 1993). Study of continuity and change in the foreign policy of the Weimar Republic and Nazi Germany.

R. F. Holt and A. Pickard, *Democracy, Dictatorship, Destruction: Documents of Modern German History 1918–45* (Longman, Australia, 1991). Useful collection of documents.

H. James, *The German Slump: Politics and Economics, 1924–36* (OUP, Oxford, 1986).

L. E. Jones, *German Liberalism and the Dissolution of the Weimar Party System* (University of North Carolina Press, USA 1988).

M. Lee and W. Michalka, *German Foreign Policy, 1917–1933* (Berg, 1987).

H. Mommsen, *From Weimar to Auschwitz* (Polity Press, 1991). A collection of detailed essays from one of Germany's foremost historians.